W9-AEH-248

SCIENCE

FOUNDATIONS

Electricity and Magnetism

SCIENCE FOUNDATIONS

SCIENCE

FOUNDATIONS

Electricity and Magnetism

KRISTI LEW

CHELSEA HOUSE
An Infobase Learning Company

Science Foundations: Electricity and Magnetism

Copyright © 2011 by Infobase Learning

Chelsea House
An imprint of Infobase Learning
132 West 31st Street
New York, NY 10001

Library of Congress Cataloging-in-Publication Data
Lew, Kristi.
  Electricity and magnetism / Kristi Lew.
     p. cm. — (Science foundations)
  Includes bibliographical references and index.
  ISBN 978-1-60413-293-9 (hardcover)
  1. Electricity—Juvenile literature. 2. Magnetism—Juvenile literature. I. Title.
  QC527.2.L49 2011
  537—dc22   2010026882

Chelsea House books are available at special discounts when purchased in bulk quantities for businesses, associations, institutions, or sales promotions. Please call our Special Sales Department in New York at (212) 967-8800 or (800) 322-8755.

You can find Chelsea House on the World Wide Web at
http://www.chelseahouse.com

Text design by Kerry Casey
Cover design by Alicia Post
Composition by EJB Publishing Services
Cover printed by Bang Printing, Brainerd, MN
Book printed and bound by Bang Printing, Brainerd, MN
Date printed: March 2011
Printed in the United States of America

10 9 8 7 6 5 4 3 2 1

This book is printed on acid-free paper.

Contents

What Is Electricity?

W e use electricity nearly every minute of every day. Our modern society relies on electric lights, clocks, air conditioners, televisions, radios, and computers. Even our bodies are driven by electricity. Without electricity, your heart would not beat, your eyes could not see, and your brain would not function. Most people do not realize how much they depend on electricity to go about their everyday lives—until the power goes out.

ELECTRIC CHARGES AND THE ATOM

To understand how electricity works, it is necessary to understand how atoms are put together. **Atoms** are the basic building blocks of all matter. **Matter** is anything that has mass and takes up space—in other words, anything that you can physically touch. A car, a desk, the air, and even you are made up of atoms.

In turn, atoms are made up of even smaller objects. These smaller objects are called subatomic particles. In most atoms, there are three main subatomic particles—**protons**, **neutrons**, and **electrons**. Protons and neutrons are found in the atom's **nucleus**. The nucleus is the dense, central core of an atom. Protons have a positive charge, but neutrons are electrically neutral. Therefore, the nucleus has an overall positive charge.

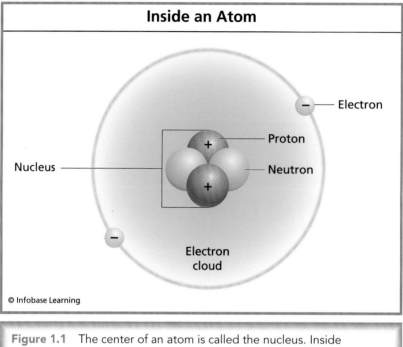

Inside an Atom

Electron

Proton

Nucleus

Neutron

Electron
cloud

© Infobase Learning

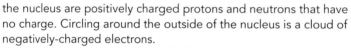

Figure 1.1 The center of an atom is called the nucleus. Inside the nucleus are positively charged protons and neutrons that have no charge. Circling around the outside of the nucleus is a cloud of negatively-charged electrons.

The last of the three main types of subatomic particles, the electrons, move around the outside of the nucleus on energy levels, or shells. Electrons are negatively charged. However, as a whole, atoms are electrically neutral. To balance out the electrically positive protons in the nucleus, therefore, atoms must contain an equal number of negatively charged electrons. Positive and negative charges are attracted to one another. This electrical attraction between positively charged protons and negatively charged electrons hold the electrons in place around an atom's nucleus. The further an electron gets from the nucleus, the weaker this attraction gets.

Electrons on an atom's outermost, or highest, energy level are the furthest away from the nucleus. These electrons are called **valence electrons**. When atoms are involved in chemical reactions, they lose, gain, or share their valence electrons.

Atoms that have lost or gained electrons are no longer neutral. If an atom loses electrons, it has more protons than electrons. Because protons have a positive charge, this creates a particle with an overall positive charge. Charged particles created by the loss or gain of electrons are called **ions**. An atom that loses electrons forms a positive ion. (A positive ion is also called a cation.) On the other hand, if an atom gains electrons, it will have more electrons than protons. In this case, a negative ion is formed. (Negative ions are also called anions.) Electrons can be transferred from one place to another, but they can never be created or destroyed. Therefore, if one atom loses an electron, another atom must gain an electron. Some materials are better at giving up their electrons, while others are better at accepting them.

STATIC ELECTRICITY

Electricity is created when charged particles, such as electrons or ions, move from one place to another. If you have ever walked across a carpeted floor in the wintertime, and then touched a metal doorknob or another person and felt a small shock as though from a flying spark, you have experienced a flow of charged particles.

When you walked across the carpet, you created a type of electricity called static electricity. Static electricity is the presence of either a positive or negative charge on the surface of an object. The friction between your shoes and the carpet causes a buildup of electric charge in your body, so when you touch another person, electrons jump from your body to your friend. These jumping electrons create a spark, shocking both of you.

Static electricity is also what causes your hair to stand on end when you pull off a wool cap. When the cap is pulled over your hair, electrons move from your hair to the wool hat. This means that each individual piece of hair now has a positive charge. Because like charges repel and each piece of hair has the same charge, each strand tries to move as far away as possible from every other strand, making your hair stick out in all directions like a fright wig!

If you pull the wool hat off of your head in a dark room, you might even be able to see sparks. A spark is caused by the movement of a stream of electrons from one object to another. You may or may not always see the spark of electricity created when you touch a doorknob or another person, but it is there all the same. Sparks of electricity are also what causes the crackling noise you may hear when you comb your hair with a plastic comb. It is easier for electrons to move from one object to another when the air is not humid. That is why you may notice more crackling and sparking and feel more shocks when you touch other people in the wintertime than in the summertime.

DISCOVERING HOW ELECTRICITY WORKS

As far back as 600 B.C., the Greek philosopher Thales of Miletus observed that if amber (fossilized tree sap) was rubbed with fur, the amber would pick up dry leaves, feathers, and small pieces of paper. Greek scientists were fascinated with amber and the static electricity that could be produced from it. In fact, some of their fascination still

Hold Tight or Let Go?

Some materials give up electrons easily when they come into contact with another material. Other types of materials are better at accepting electrons. Scientists have made a list that ranks materials according to their tendency to give up or take in electrons. This list is called the triboelectric series. The higher a material is on the list, the more likely it will give up its electrons and become positively charged.

The relative position of two materials on the list shows how they will react with each other. If, for example, a wool hat is pulled over human hair, the hair will acquire a positive charge because it is above wool on the triboelectric series. In turn, the wool will acquire a negative charge. If the wool hat is rubbed over a piece of amber or a rubber balloon, however, the wool hat will become positively charged while the amber or the balloon becomes negatively charged.

lingers in our language. Words that begin with *electr-*, such as *electron*, *electricity*, and *electronics*, for example, come from the Greek word *electron*, which means "amber."

Later, people found other substances, such as glass, rubber, and plastic, that could be charged like amber. In the early eighteenth century, scientists called those objects that could be charged "electrics." For example, they knew that, like amber, a hard rubber rod could be electrified by rubbing it with a piece of fur, and that glass could be electrified by rubbing it with silk. They also realized that glass showed opposite properties to amber when it was electrified. This convinced scientists of the time that there were two different types of electrics. Because these two different types had different properties, scientists found that two charged rubber rods, for example, would repel each other, but that a rubber rod and a glass rod were attracted to each other. At the time, scientists did not believe that all substances could be electrified. They named the substances that could not be charged "non-electrics."

Table 1.1: The Triboelectric Series	
Positive materials (most likely to give up electrons)	Air Human skin Rabbit fur Glass Human hair Nylon Wool
Neutral materials (do not give up or take in electrons easily)	Paper Cotton Wood
Negative materials (most likely to accept electrons)	Amber Rubber balloon Hard rubber rod Mylar balloon Metals (copper, silver, gold, etc.) Plastics Silicon

In 1733, however, French chemist Charles DuFay (1698–1739) proved that all substances, not just some of them, could be electrified. (Although, DuFay also realized that some things certainly were easier to electrify than others.) DuFay named the type of charge produced on a glass rod a vitreous charge. The type of charge developed by resinous materials, such as rubber and amber, he called resinous. DuFay also observed that objects electrified with the same type of charge repelled each other while those that had opposite types of charges attracted each other. Later, two people, Benjamin Franklin (1706–1790) and William Watson (1715–1787) would independently change DuFay's terms for the different types of charges to positive and negative.

BENJAMIN FRANKLIN AND ELECTRICITY

In America, a little over a decade after DuFay's experiments with electricity were published, Benjamin Franklin took up the study of electricity. From previous experiments by other scientists, Franklin knew that when two substances, such as glass and silk, for example, are rubbed together, a charge could be transferred from one object to the other. Franklin determined that in order for one object to become positively charged, it must take what he called "fire" from the other object. Today, scientists know that Franklin's fire is really made up of electrons, but Franklin conducted his experiments long before the electron was discovered by Joseph John Thomson (1856–1940) in 1897.

Even though Franklin did not know exactly what was happening on the atomic level, his observation that a substance could be transferred from one object to another when they are rubbed together was correct. Today, scientists know that if one object gives up electrons to become positively charged, the electrons that the object casts off cannot just disappear. They must go somewhere else. Where do they go? They attach themselves to another object. When Franklin rubbed a glass rod with a silk cloth, for example, the glass transferred electrons to the silk. Because the glass gave away some of its electrons, it became positively charged. In turn, the silk accepted electrons from the glass to become negatively charged. This idea is called the theory of conservation of charge.

Figure 1.2   A lithograph depicts Benjamin Franklin and his son William using a kite and key during a storm to prove that lightning was electricity in June 1752.

Flying a Kite

Benjamin Franklin's interest in electricity was not confined to just glass and silk. When Franklin's name is mentioned, many people form a mental image of a kite being flown during an electrical storm. Indeed, during a thunderstorm in June 1752, Franklin did, apparently, carry out this incredibly dangerous experiment. Luckily for him, a lightning bolt did not actually strike his kite. If it had, it might very well have been the last thing the great man did. In fact, two men who tried the same experiment after Franklin were both electrocuted and killed.

Although Franklin's kite was not directly hit by lightning, it did pick up electrical charges from the storm clouds. These charges traveled down the wet kite string and through a metal key. When

Franklin held his hand close enough to the metal key, sparks flew, proving that lightning was, indeed, made of electric charges.

Scientists today know a little bit more about what causes lightning strikes than they did during Franklin's time. However, there is still a lot that they do not know. A lightning strike begins when two air masses rub together. This happens a lot in the summertime when warm, wet air rises from the ground and meets a layer of cooler, drier air above. The rubbing of the air masses charges the clouds. This is the reason there are more thunderstorms in the summertime than in the winter when air masses are drier. The exact mechanism causing the clouds to get charged up, however, is still up for debate within the scientific community.

One theory is that atoms near the tops of the clouds lose electrons and become positively charged. Atoms near the bottom of the cloud, on the other hand, accept the cast-off electrons and become negatively charged. When the difference in the number of electrons becomes large enough, electrons move rapidly from the cloud and zigzag toward the surface of the earth. These zigzags of negative charge are invisible to the human eye. Scientists call the zigzagging packets of electrons stepped leaders.

When a stepped leader gets close enough to the ground, it repels the electrons in the ground or objects on (or near) the ground. Because the electrons in the ground or object are repelled, that area of ground or that side of the object closest to the stepped leader acquires a positive charge.

When enough positive charges build up, the positive charges attract the negative charges and they connect. When the charges

St. Elmo's Fire

The buildup of charge in some objects, especially around tall, pointed objects such as church steeples, sailboat masts, and lightning rods, can sometimes be seen. Scientists call the weak light produced around these objects coronal discharge, but the phenomenon is more commonly known as St. Elmo's fire.

Figure 1.3 Forked lightning typically refers to cloud-to-ground lightning that has a branched path.

meet, a cloud-to-ground connection is made. This connection triggers what scientists call a return stroke. In a return stroke, electrons flow along a path of ionized air made by the stepped leader to create a visible path—a flash of lightning. The buildup of charges, which creates a cloud-to-ground connection, and the flash of a return stroke may sound like it takes a long time, but it can all happen in thousandths of a second. The familiar forked appearance of a lightning bolt is caused by the steps that the stepped leader takes to reach the ground.

A tremendous amount of energy is produced with the flow of electrons in a return stroke. This energy not only produces light so that we can see the lightning bolt, it also produces heat—and a lot of it. In fact, a lightning bolt can heat the air around it to more than 45,032°F (25,000°C)—hotter than the surface of the Sun! The huge surge of energy released when lightning strikes the ground also compresses the air around the lightning bolt, producing a shock-wave. The shockwave is conducted through the air where it eventually hits our ears and we hear thunder.

Lightning Protection and Grounding

Lightning tends to strike taller objects—sailboat masts, church steeples, and New York City's Empire State Building, for example—more often than shorter ones. Taller objects get hit more often simply because they bring the ground closer to the clouds. And the stepped leader is looking for the easiest, fastest path to ground.

Franklin noticed this tendency, so he also invented the lightning rod. A lightning rod is usually a tall, pointed piece of metal attached to a wire that leads to the surface of the earth, providing a good conductive path to the ground. Because lightning rods conduct electricity well, they provide protection to objects that are not as conductive, such as houses and buildings.

Lightning can also use your body to connect to the ground. Every year, more than 1,000 Americans are struck by lightning. To prevent this from happening, the best thing to do when a thunderstorm approaches is to take shelter in a house or car. If this is not possible, avoid standing or sitting under trees. Because water conducts electricity better than air, trees, which contain water and sap, provide a good conductive path to the ground. And because of their height, trees make great natural lightning rods. Do not lie down on the ground either. This position makes you a larger target. Instead, put your feet very close together, crouch down, and tuck your head. Make your body as small as possible without touching the ground.

Even if you are inside a house, lightning can pose a danger. If lightning strikes a house, it can set the house on fire. It can also travel through metal pipes and wires. So avoid touching metal plumbing fixtures and using corded telephones. Luckily, of the more than 1,000 people struck by lightning each year in the United States, about 90% of them survive their ordeal—but not without lingering scars and disabilities.

Conductors and Insulators

Franklin's experiments with the kite and lightning are not the only investigations he conducted with electricity. He also noted that some substances would allow electric charges to move from one place to another. Today, scientists call a substance that exhibits this property a **conductor**. Conductors allow streams of electrons or ions to flow through them easily. This means that conductors can transfer electricity from one place to another. The copper wires in your house, for example, are good conductors. They allow the electricity coming from the electrical power plant to flow through them and into your home.

Conductors can do this because they contain some electrons that are not tightly bound to an individual atom. These unattached electrons can move easily through the conductor. Nonconductors, on the other hand, do not have free-floating electrons. All of their electrons are fixed in their individual atoms.

Metals, like copper, for example, tend to have a lot of these free-floating electrons. The electrons on the outermost, or highest, energy level of a metallic atom are free to move through the metal. As an example, picture a metal as a handful of marbles surrounded by water. The marbles represent the metal atoms that have lost their valence electrons. Because the metal atoms have lost their valence electrons, they are actually a group of positively charged ions. In metals, these cations have a special name: kernels. The kernels are surrounded by a sea of electrons. In fact, the valence electrons moving around the kernels are similar to the water moving around marbles.

Metals are held together by the attraction between the positively charged kernels and the negatively charged electron sea. This type

Metallic Properties

The nature of a metallic bond also explains why metals dent rather than break when they are pounded. When a metal is smacked by a hammer, for example, its kernels can slide around in their sea of electrons. The ability of metals to be hammered into a sheet or bent into a shape is a property called malleability. Another property of metals is the ability to be drawn into wires. This property is called ductile. Both properties exist in metals because of the special metallic bond between metal atoms.

of attraction is called a metallic bond. Because of their free-floating electrons, most metals are very good electrical conductors. Liquids that contain free-flowing ions make good conductors, too. Most tap water, for example, contains ions from dissolved minerals and salts, so it conducts electricity well.

Glass and rubber, on the other hand, do not allow charges to move through them very easily. Therefore, glass and rubber are good **insulators**. Plastic, wood, air, and purified water (also called distilled or deionized water because it contains no dissolved ions) are all good insulators, too. Unlike metals, these substances do not conduct electricity very well because their valence electrons are held fairly tightly in individual atoms and are not free to move around.

If an object is going to conduct electricity, it needs to be insulated. Otherwise, all of the charges would just flow away, like water down a drain. Insulators act as drain stoppers. They prevent streams of charges from flowing out. This is the reason that most electrical wires you come into contact with every day are wrapped in plastic. The metal in the electrical wires is a conductor. It allows charges to flow through the wires. The plastic wrapped around the metal wires is an insulator. It prevents the charges from flowing through you when you pick up a cord plugged into a wall socket. That's a good thing. Otherwise, you might end up getting a nasty shock.

How Does
Electricity Work?

Electricity is not only used to power our lights, computers, and refrigerators. It powers our bodies, too. However, our bodies do not contain metal wires for electrons to flow through. Instead of using flowing electrons to convey an electrical signal, our bodies use a different kind of charged particle—an ion. Remember that an ion is formed when an atom attains an electrical charge by losing or gaining electrons.

BIOELECTRICITY

The human body uses ions to relay messages from the brain to the nerves. The nerves pass on these messages from the brain to other parts of the body by moving the ions along nerve cells. Nerves relay messages from other parts of the body like the eyes, ears, nose, skin, and muscles back to the brain, too. The moving ions produce little pulses of electricity. These electrical signals can zing along chains of nerve cells at a speed of 224 miles (360 kilometers) per hour.

Even though nerve impulses speed along fairly rapidly, the heart cannot wait to receive an electrical signal from the brain in order to beat. Instead, a group of cells near the heart produces its own electrical impulses to tell the heart muscle when to contract and when to relax. The frequency, or pace, of these impulses is controlled by the brain. As people get older, this group of cells sometimes loses its ability to tell the heart when to beat. When this happens, doctors may suggest inserting a pacemaker. (A pacemaker is a tiny device placed inside the body near the heart that delivers a small electric shock to regulate the heartbeat.) Without this group of cells, or an artificial pacemaker, the heart would stop beating as it should and the person would die.

Because the human body is a good electrical conductor, an electric shock from a downed power line, a car battery, or an electrical outlet in the home could interfere with the body's natural electrical signals—sometimes with devastating consequences. Depending on the source of electricity and how long a person is in contact with it, injuries can be as mild as a slight tingling sensation to as severe as death. However, not all electric shocks are bad. A defibrillator, for example, can be a real lifesaver. If someone's heart is not beating properly (or not beating at all), this device can send a brief electric shock though their heart and restore the heartbeat to normal.

JUMPING FROG LEGS AND THE BATTERY

Like other animals, frogs are great electrical conductors. The Italian scientist Luigi Galvani (1737–1798) discovered this fact in 1782 while dissecting a few frogs near an apparatus called a Leyden jar, a device that stores electric charges. When Galvani moved the frogs' legs close to the Leyden jar, the electric charges caused the legs to jump.

About a decade later, in the early 1790s, Alessandro Volta (1745–1827) repeated Galvani's experiments with frog legs. He was also able to make the legs jump, but then he decided to try the experiment again without the frog's legs and experiment on himself instead. When he put a piece of copper on one side of his tongue and a piece of zinc on the other side, he felt a tingling sensation when he touched the two metal pieces together. Volta actually made electricity in his mouth! This was, basically, the first battery. Even though a battery in the mouth is not all that useful, the experiment nevertheless gave Volta an idea of how a battery needed to be constructed.

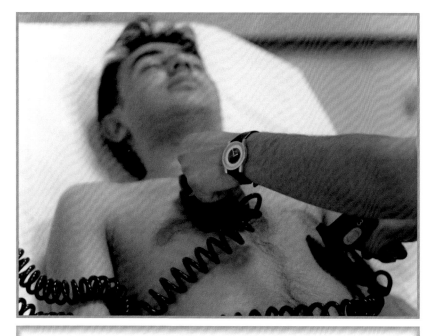

Figure 2.1 A defibrillator is used to send a dose of electrical energy to restore the rhythm to an irregular or weakened heartbeat.

After many experiments, Volta discovered that all he really needed to produce electricity was two different metals and a moist conductor. To make the first practical battery, Volta made a pile of about 20 alternating silver and zinc disks. Now, he needed a moist conductor. Because frog legs and saliva are not the most convenient experimental materials, Volta decided to replace them with cloth soaked in salt water. He put a piece of this cloth between each disk. When he used a wire to connect the silver disk at the top of the pile with the bottom zinc disk, he found that a steady supply of electricity flowed through the pile.

All the batteries that are in use today are based on the principles first discovered by Volta. The terminal ends of the pile became known as **electrodes**. The electrodes, or the terminals, of a battery are the points where electrons enter or leave the battery. Between the two terminals, batteries produce a difference in potential energy.

POTENTIAL ENERGY

An object that is not moving but that has the potential to move contains **potential energy**. For example, a ball sitting at the top of a hill contains gravitational potential energy because gravity can cause the ball to move down the hill. When the ball begins to move, its potential energy is converted into **kinetic energy**, the energy of motion. Charges can also contain potential energy. If, for example, a positive charge is in some position in space and another positive charge comes close to it, the charge has the potential to move the second positive charge away. The second charge also has the potential to move the first one. Both charges possess electric potential energy.

Animal Electricity

Humans are not the only animals that have nerves constantly firing off electricity. All animals do. Some animals, however, would no doubt like to be able to shut this bodily function off every now and then. Fish and other animals in the sea, for example, are constantly shuffling ions back and forth, giving off tiny, invisible electric pulses. Much to their distress, these electrical signals can be detected by sharks. No matter how quietly fish sit on the ocean bottom trying to avoid detection, if their brains and hearts are still working, they are sending the shark signals just as clearly as if they were waving their fins and frantically shouting the fishy equivalent of "Here I am! Over here! Come get me!"

Sharks are not the only animals that use electricity. Electric eels do, too, but in a different way. An electric eel's body contains special cells that can generate and store electricity similar to the way a battery can. When the eel is threatened or when they find a fish they want to eat, the eel can discharge these cells all at once, producing a burst of electricity five times more powerful than the electricity that

Charges naturally move from areas of high electric potential energy to areas of low potential, just like a ball naturally rolls down a hill (an area with lower gravitational potential energy) instead of up (an area with higher potential energy). Once the potential energy difference is equalized, the charges will no longer flow.

This is the reason birds can sit on high-voltage electrical wires without going up in flames. As long as the bird's two feet are on the same wire, there is no potential difference. As long as there is no potential difference, the bird is safe. However, as soon as one foot touches another piece of metal, like the pole holding the high-voltage wire, there is a difference in voltage, and electricity can flow between the two pieces of metal through the bird. Too much potential difference and—POOF!—cooked bird.

Figure 2.2   To aid in hunting and self-defense, an electric eel is able to generate powerful electric shocks. It generates the electrical pulse in a way similar to a battery, and just one shock—with 500 watts (1 ampere) of current—could kill a human.

comes out of a standard U.S. wall socket. The poor fish on the receiving end of the electric eel's shocking talent has, essentially, been Tasered.

To keep electrons flowing, there must be a potential difference between two points. Batteries create a potential energy difference between the two terminals. This potential energy difference keeps the charges and, therefore, the electricity, flowing.

COULOMB'S LAW

About the same time Luigi Galvani was using a Leyden jar to make frog legs jump, another scientist, Charles Coulomb (1736–1806), became interested in measuring the strength of the forces of attraction and repulsion between two charges. To make these measurements, Coulomb reinvented a piece of equipment called a torsion balance. The first torsion balance was invented by John Mitchell (1724–1793),

Fruity Electricity

You can make your own battery with two lemons, two pennies, two nails, and some copper wire. Wrap a length of copper wire around one penny and a different bit of copper wire around one of the nails. Take a third length of wire and wrap one end around the remaining penny and the other end around the remaining nail. Cut a slit in each lemon (be sure to first get permission from an adult before using the knife).

Place the penny wrapped in copper wire into one of the slots you cut into one of the lemons. Into the same lemon, stick the nail attached to the second penny.

Now take the second lemon and slide the penny attached to the nail into the slot you cut. Put the remaining nail into this second lemon, too. You should now have two lemons, each with one penny and one nail stuck into it. If you touch the free ends of the two copper wires to your tongue, you should be able to feel a small tingle—just like Volta did.

an English geologist, who intended to use the instrument to measure the Earth's gravity. However, the device was not widely known until Coulomb invented his own version to measure electrostatic charges.

Using his torsion balance, Coulomb discovered that larger charges attract and repel each other with more force than smaller charges. He also found that the force between two charges is stronger the closer together they are. After many experiments, Coulomb came to the conclusion that the force of attraction or repulsion between two charges is directly proportional to the product of their charges and inversely proportional to the square of the distance between the charges. The mathematical equation that describes what Coulomb found looks like this:

$$F = k\frac{q_1 \times q_2}{r^2}$$

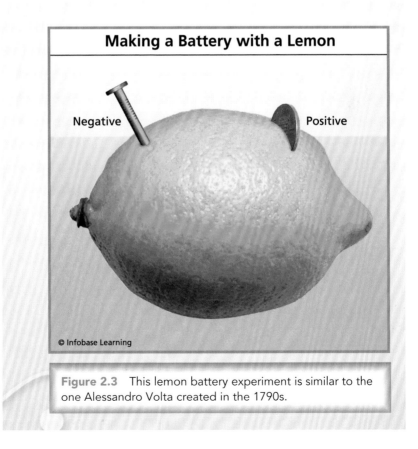

Making a Battery with a Lemon

Negative

Positive

© Infobase Learning

Figure 2.3   This lemon battery experiment is similar to the one Alessandro Volta created in the 1790s.

In this equation, the letter F stands for force, r is the distance between the charges, q_1 is the numerical value of one of the charges, and q_2 is the magnitude of the other charge. The letter k is called the electrostatic constant or Coulomb's constant. It is equal to

$$8.98 \times 10^9 N \times m^2/C^2$$

If the two charges are both positive or if they are both negative, their product will be a positive number. Therefore, if the numerical value of F is positive, the two charges repel each other. On the other hand, if the two charges have opposite charges (one positive and one negative), their product will be a negative number. A negative F value indicates an attractive force.

Because the force of attraction or repulsion is directly proportional to the product of the charges, larger charges exert more force. The equation also shows that force is inversely proportional to the square of the distance between the charges. This means that if, for example, the distance between two charges is doubled, the force between them decreases by a factor of 4 (the square of 2). If the distance is tripled, the force is decreased by a factor of 9 (the square of 3), and so on.

Even though this idea was independently discovered by two other scientists, John Robison (1739–1805) and Henry Cavendish (1731–1810), at the same time that Coulomb was working on it, it has become known as Coulomb's law. In physics, Coulomb's law is called an inverse square law, but it is not the only inverse square law in physics. Newton's law of gravitational attraction is an inverse square law, too.

ELECTRIC FIELDS

About 50 years later, another scientist, Michael Faraday (1791–1867), picked up Coulomb's work on the forces between two electrically charged particles. In 1844, Faraday developed the idea that all charges are surrounded by what he called lines of force. Today, physicists call these lines of force an electric field.

Like Coulomb, Faraday found that the larger the charge, the more powerful the attractive or repulsive force exerted by the charge. Faraday determined that this means that a larger charge has a stronger electric field surrounding it. The electric field around a single charged particle, such as a proton, for example, stretches out into the empty space around the charge. If an electron moves inside the proton's electric field, it is pulled toward the proton (because unlike charges are attracted to each other).

Luckily for us, the attraction between protons and electrons is a strong one, much stronger than the gravitational force that keeps us rooted to the earth. In fact, the electrical attraction between an electron and a proton is 10^{39} times stronger (that is 1,000 trillion trillion trillion times stronger) than the gravitational force between them. Good thing, too. This electrical attraction keeps electrons

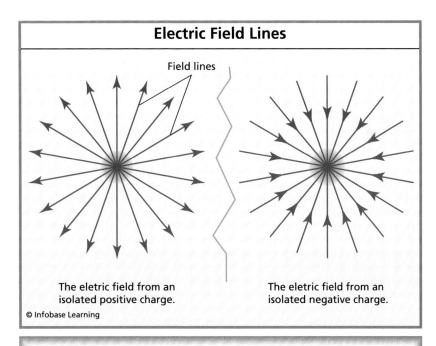

Electric Field Lines

Field lines

The eletric field from an isolated positive charge.

The eletric field from an isolated negative charge.

© Infobase Learning

Figure 2.4 Electric field lines illustrate how the electric field would change based on whether a particle is given a negative or a positive charge.

orbiting the nuclei of atoms. It also holds atoms together in molecules and holds molecules together in liquids and solids. Without electrical attraction, atoms (and, therefore, all matter) would just fall apart.

By convention, physicists today draw electric field lines around a charged particle to show how the electric field would affect a positive charge. A positive charge would be drawn with the lines of force directed outward, away from the charge because it would exert a repulsive force on another positive charge. Negative charges, on the other hand, have lines of force directed inward as they would exert an attractive force on a positive charge. The spacing of field lines drawn by a physicist is important, too. The strength of the electric field is represented by the distance between the field lines—the

Van de Graaff Generators

The easiest (and most fun) way to see an electric field in action is to use a Van de Graaff generator. Invented by Massachusetts Institute of Technology (MIT) professor Robert Van de Graaff (1901–1967), a Van de Graaff generator creates electric charges. Generating electric charges inside this kind of generator often involves the use of two rollers—one made of nylon and one made of silicon. When a motor is turned on, the two rollers rub against each other. Because nylon is higher on the triboelectric series than silicon is, the nylon acquires a positive charge while the silicon roller is negatively charged. In turn, the nylon roller transfers its positive charges to the surface of a large sphere that makes up the exterior of a Van de Graaff generator. When someone touches the sphere of the Van de Graaff generator, each strand of that person's hair acquires a positive charge and stands up on end. The effect is much like dragging a wool cap off of your head.

Van de Graaff generators can be used to create sparks, too. To do this, two side-by-side Van de Graaff generators, one generating a positive charge and the other a negative closer the field lines, the stronger the field and the stronger the attractive or repulsive force.

Sparks and lightning are caused by very strong electric fields. Both of these phenomena occur when an electric field is strong enough to ionize, or rip electrons off, atoms in the air. Ionized air is also called *plasma*. Unlike non-ionized air, plasma contains electrons that are free to move around. Just like the free-floating electrons in metals make them good electrical conductors, the free-floating electrons in plasma make it a good conductor, too. Ionized air can conduct electricity much like a metal wire does. When ionized air conducts electricity, it gets hot enough to glow white-hot. When we see sparks or lightning, we are seeing ionized air conduct electricity.

Figure 2.5 A woman's hair is electrified as she touches a Van de Graaff generator to promote the International Trade Fair for Energy on January 23, 2009, in Leipzig, Germany.

charge, are needed. When the electric field between the two generators becomes large enough to ionize air, a "lightning bolt" shoots across the space between the two spheres.

Electric Currents and Circuits

Sparks and lightning are caused by a buildup of positive and negative charges on the surface of an object. These charges are static (remain in place) until the imbalance becomes so great that they discharge, sometimes in a dramatic fashion, such as a lightning bolt. In some circumstances, static electricity can be useful. Some types of air filters have an electrostatic charge and are used to attract dust particles, for example. However, this type of electricity is not useful for powering our modern electronic devices. To produce the type of electricity that is supplied by a wall socket like the ones in our homes, scientists had to learn how to harness moving charges.

CURRENTS

In supplying electricity to our homes, electrons flow through the wires in a manner that is similar to the way water flows down a riverbed. Because of this similarity, the flow of electrons through a wire is called an electric **current**. An electric current is the movement of electric charges from one place to another. The speed at which an electric current moves from one point to another depends on the potential difference between the two points. Just as water pressure forces water through a pipe, potential difference pushes a current of flowing electrons through a wire.

Current is a measure of the number of electrons (or other charged particles) that flow past a certain point over a certain time period. The unit that physicists use to measure electric charges is called a coulomb. Therefore, current is measured in coulombs per second. Another name for coulombs per second is amperes (commonly called an amp).

One amp of current is equal to 6 quintillion (6,000,000,000,000, 000,000) electrons flowing past a spot in the wire in one second. A standard household light bulb will light up when one amp worth of electrons flows through household wires. A car's starter motor, on the other hand, must supply 50 amps, or 300 quintillion electrons every second, to a car's spark plugs in order for the car to start.

The strength of the force that pushes these electrons along is measured in volts. The voltage a battery can produce depends on the types of metals and the type of moist conductor, called the **electrolyte**, that are used in the battery. The frog legs, saliva, and saltwater used by Volta, for example, would each produce different voltages if they were used in batteries. An electrolyte is any substance that produces ions and is capable of conducting electricity when it is dissolved in water or melted. Instead of frog legs, saliva, or saltwater, most batteries today use sulfuric acid (for car batteries) or lithium salts dissolved in a solvent (for rechargeable batteries) as an electrolyte. When a battery's terminals are connected to an electrical circuit, a chemical reaction takes place. This chemical reaction causes the metal atoms that make up the battery's electrodes to give up their electrons. The positive ions that result from this chemical reaction flow through the electrolyte. The electrons flow through the electrical circuit, providing the electricity needed.

Any kind of moving charge, positive or negative, will cause a current of electricity. When scientists began their study of electricity, they believed that the charges moving through metals were positive. Only later did they determine that the charges moving through metals are actually free electrons and, therefore, negative. By the time they had this figured out, however, the convention to show current as the flow of positive charge was already set. Therefore, if positive ions are flowing to the right in a liquid the current is also shown flowing to the right. If electrons are moving along a metal wire, however, the current is shown moving in the opposite direction.

OHM'S LAW

Some materials allow electrons to flow through them easier than other materials. The degree to which a material slows the flow of electrons is called its **resistance**. A material's resistance to the flow of electrons depends on the atomic structure of the material. Metals,

Electrolysis and Electroplating

Not long after Volta made the first battery, English scientists William Nicholson (1753–1815) and Anthony Carlisle (1768–1840) discovered that if an electric current was passed though water, the water would break down into hydrogen and oxygen, the elements that make it up. This procedure is called electrolysis.

Michael Faraday did quite a lot of work with electrolysis. He found that an electric current would flow easily through some liquids, such as saltwater and sulfuric acid, for example, but not through others, such as sugar water. Scientists now know that this is because sulfuric acid and sodium chloride (salt) break down into ions when they are dissolved in water, but sugar does not. Faraday named aqueous solutions (a solution in which the solvent is water) that conduct electricity electrolytes. Those solutions that do not conduct electricity are called nonelectrolytes.

Faraday also noticed that if the electrolyte he used contained metal ions, the ions would be deposited on one of the battery's electrodes. Today, this process is known as electroplating. Electroplating is often used to deposit a thin layer of one metal over another to provide particular properties. Zinc, for example, is often used to plate steel. The zinc coating prevents the steel from rusting.

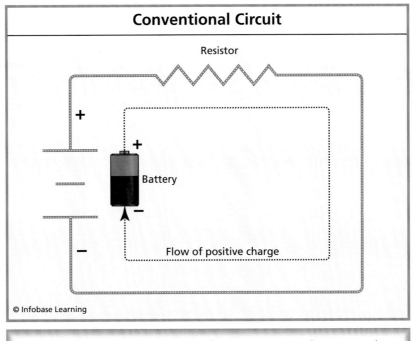

Conventional Circuit

Resistor

+

+

Battery

−

Flow of positive charge

−

© Infobase Learning

Figure 3.1 This illustration depicts how a conventional current works with a positive charge flowing across the wire.

for example, have little resistance (and are, therefore, good conductors) because of their free-floating electrons.

Temperature also plays a role in resistance. When the temperature of a material increases, the random movement of the atoms in that material also increases. This random movement interferes with the flow of current, increasing the resistance of the material. Lowering the temperature, on the other hand, lowers the resistance. In fact, there are some materials, called **superconductors**, that, at a low-enough temperature, have almost no resistance to electrical current. With the exception of superconductors, however, almost all materials resist the flow of current to some extent.

Resistance is measured in units known as **ohms**. The unit is named in honor of the German physicist Georg Ohm (c.1789–1854) who discovered the relationship between voltage, current, and resistance. Through his experiments, Ohm discovered two important things. First, the strength of the electrical current that a wire can carry is proportional to the diameter of the wire, inversely proportional to the length of the wire, and dependent on the material used to make the wire. In other words, a thicker wire can carry more current. The further away you move from the source of the current, the weaker the current becomes. In addition, some materials, such as metals, carry current much better than other substances.

The second important discovery that Ohm made is that the current is directly proportional to the voltage and inversely proportional to the resistance in the wire. This means that an increase in voltage increases the current, but when a current encounters resistance, the flow slows down. This is similar to how the flow of water slows down if a pipe gets narrower.

The relationship that Ohm discovered between voltage (V), current (I), and resistance (R) can be shown mathematically like this:

$$V = IR$$

This relationship is known as Ohm's law. Because the current in a wire is directly proportional to the voltage supplied, if the voltage doubles (while the resistance stays the same), the current will also double. On the other hand, the current is inversely proportional to the resistance. Therefore, if the resistance is doubled (while keeping the voltage the same), the current going through the wire will be cut in half.

The more current that flows though a wire, the more heat it generates. Toasters, for example, have wires that allow a large current to pass though them with low resistance. This creates enough heat to toast bread. In fact, many electrical devices are controlled by controlling resistance. The volume control knob on a speaker, for example, lowers the resistance when the knob is turned up, allowing more current to flow and resulting in a louder volume.

A light bulb is another common device that relies on controlling resistance. The filament in a light bulb is a tiny, thin wire that presents a lot of resistance. When current is forced though such a small wire, the filament heats up so much that it glows white-hot and gives off light. This heating, called ohmic heating, occurs in any conductor that has even a small amount of resistance. Filaments in light bulbs are made thin on purpose to take advantage of ohmic heating. So are the elements in toasters and electric space heaters. However, ohmic heating must be taken into account when delivering electricity from power plants to homes. Wire thicknesses

Figure 3.2   German physicist Georg Ohm's experiments helped him to define the fundamental relationship between voltage, current, and resistance, which is considered to be the first step in electrical circuit analysis.

must be chosen carefully to prevent overheating, too. Overheated wires can melt through the insulation surrounding them and cause combustible material such as furniture or draperies to catch on fire. The wires in the walls that lead up to the filament in a light bulb, for example, are much thicker so that they stay cooler than the filament. Any conductor (other than superconductors) will lose some energy to ohmic heating.

POWER

An object's potential energy is its capacity for doing work due to its position. Physicists define work as moving an object from one place to another by applying a force. Batteries, for example, provide the force that moves electrons though the wires in a flashlight. Because the battery is causing the electrons to move though some distance, it can be said that work is being done on the electrons by the battery. This movement changes the electron's potential energies. This change between the original potential energy state of an electron and its final potential energy state is called the potential difference. Voltage is the measurement of electric potential difference.

Power is the rate at which work is done. A **watt** is a measurement of energy over time, or a measurement of power (P). The power output of a power supply (like a battery) is proportional to the current it is supplying. In other words, the higher the power output, the larger the current. The mathematical formula that describes the relationship between power, current, and voltage is:

$$P = IV$$

Physicists use this equation along with Ohm's law to calculate many different values. For example, imagine that you needed to know the resistance in a 150-watt light bulb. The unit watt is a measurement of power, so you know that P = 150 watts. The voltage coming through a standard household wall outlet is 120 volts, so V = 120 volts. To find out how much current is flowing through the filament of the light bulb, solve the equation for I.

$$I = P/V = 150 \text{ watts}/120 \text{ volts} =$$
$$1.25 \text{ watts/volts or } 1.25 \text{ amps of current}$$

Remember that the relationship between current and resistance is given by the formula V = IR. Therefore, to find out the resistance, solve this equation for R.

$$R = V/I = 120 \text{ volts}/1.25 \text{ amps} =$$
96 volts/amps or 96 ohms of resistance

The voltage written on a battery is a measure of the potential difference between the battery's two terminals. Car batteries, for example, are usually rated at 12 volts (V). Double A (AA) batteries are usually 1.5 V. Depending on what type of electronic device you want to use them in, two or more AAs (or other type of battery) may be needed to provide the power for the device to run. As long as a battery is functional, it will supply the same amount of current all the time.

CIRCUITS

An electric current will flow through a light bulb, radio, or other electric device only if there is an electric field to push the charges though a **circuit**. A circuit is a pathway that consists of a power supply (such as a battery), some wires, and a resistor (such as the light

AC and DC

There are two major types of current—direct current (DC) and alternating current (AC). In a DC, electrons move steadily in one direction over a period of time. Batteries are a source of direct current.

AC power supplies are much more common. The current that comes into homes and business, for example, is AC. An alternating current flows one way for a certain period of time and then it changes direction. In the United States and Canada, AC power alternates at 60 cycles per second. That means that the direction of current between the two slots in a wall outlet alternates back and forth 60 times per second. The unit for cycles per second is called a hertz (Hz). The 60 Hz AC power delivered to your home has a voltage of 120 V.

bulb). The battery of a flashlight, for example, provides the electric field that makes electrons flow through the flashlight bulb. In order for a circuit to carry an electric current, there must be a continuous loop for the electrons to flow through. In the flashlight charges flow from one terminal of the battery, through the flashlight wires and the light bulb, and back to the other terminal of the battery. This loop is called a closed circuit.

A light bulb in one of the rooms of your house works much the same way. When you walk into a dark room and flip on the light switch, the switch closes a circuit. When the circuit closes, electrons

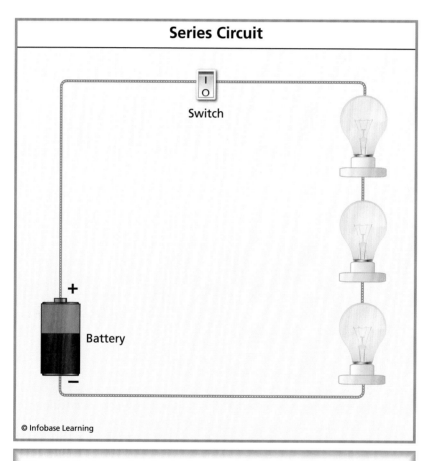

Series Circuit

Switch

Battery

© Infobase Learning

Figure 3.3 In a series circuit, the current is the same throughout. They use less wiring than parallel circuits, and they are useful in providing a warning if one component in a circuit has failed.

Parallel Circuits

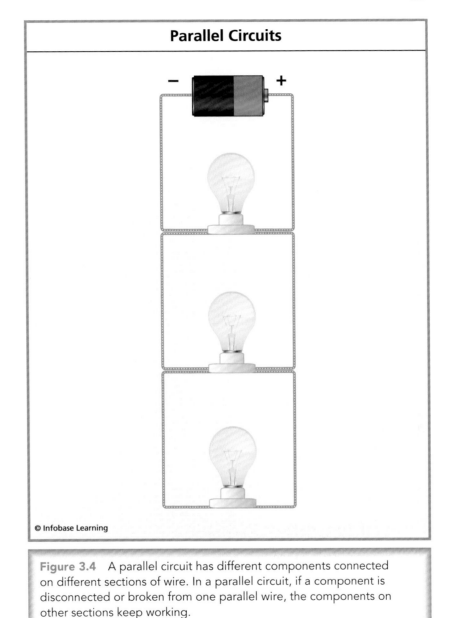

© Infobase Learning

Figure 3.4 A parallel circuit has different components connected on different sections of wire. In a parallel circuit, if a component is disconnected or broken from one parallel wire, the components on other sections keep working.

flow through wires in the walls of the room to the light bulb in the overhead light. The electrons then flow through the bulb's filament. The resistance in the tiny wire causes it to heat up and glow white-hot, giving off light. If the bulb's filament breaks, the light bulb "burns out." Because the electrons cannot travel though a broken filament, the circuit is broken and the bulb will not light and must be changed for one that does not have a broken filament. The bulb will also stop producing light if you flip off the light switch because the circuit is no longer closed. In this case, however, the circuit is not really broken. You can close the circuit again and make the light bulb go back on by simply flipping the light switch back into the on position and allowing the electrons to flow again.

There are two types of circuits—series and parallel. The simplest type of circuit is a series circuit. All you need to make a series circuit is a voltage source (like a battery), a resistance or a load (a light bulb, for example), and a wire to connect and carry the current between them. In a series circuit, current must flow through one component (the light bulb, for example) before it can move on to another component. This means that if the circuit has multiple light bulbs, the electric current must flow through one light bulb before

What Is a Short Circuit?

A short circuit occurs when a connection with low resistance is made between the terminals of a power supply, such as when a wire touches the two terminals of a battery. Short circuits are usually accidental and allow current to flow along an unintended path (usually a shorter one, hence the name). Because of the low resistance, a very large current flow is forced through the circuit. Large currents create a lot of heat. Short circuits in a home are very dangerous because they can easily set the house on fire.

Not all short circuits are accidental, however. In fact, some are quite useful. One practical use of a short circuit is in arc welding. An arc welding machine can supply a very large current to the welding rod. Welders touch a welding rod to two metals that they want to fuse together. The large current flows through the metals, heating them up so much that they melt together into one solid, fused piece.

moving on to the next. Because of the way a series circuit is wired, if one of the bulbs burns out, the entire circuit is broken and all of the lights go out. Older Christmas tree lights were often strung in a series circuit.

Parallel circuits, on the other hand, are wired to prevent this problem. In a parallel circuit, the current can flow though any component in the circuit independent of any other components. In other words, the current does not need to go through one light bulb to get to another bulb. Imagine a water pipe that comes to a junction and splits into two pipes, for example. Some of the water goes through one pipe while some water goes through the other. The current does the same thing in a parallel circuit. Circuits in today's electronics are rarely just series circuits or just parallel circuits, but a complicated combination of the two.

4

What Is Magnetism?

Electricity is not the only useful invisible force that surrounds us everyday. Magnets are all around you, too, even if you cannot always see them. Magnets can be found in stereo speakers, computers, tape recorders, on the backs of credit cards, in our car motors, telephones, and, of course, to hold those cute, little, hand-drawn pictures up on the refrigerator.

WHAT IS MAGNETISM?

Magnetism is the natural ability of some materials to attract iron. The Greek philosopher Thales of Miletus not only discovered that rubbing amber with fur caused it to pick up dust and feathers, he was also the first to observe that lodestone could attract pieces of iron. Originally, Thales believed that rubbing the amber made it magnetic, but when he tested this idea, the amber would not pick up the pieces of iron like the lodestone did. (As previously noted, Thales had discovered static electricity by rubbing the amber with the fur, but he did not discover magnetism.)

Lodestone is one of the varieties of a mineral called magnetite. Magnetite is an iron ore. It is the most magnetic of all minerals on Earth. In fact, all types of magnetite are naturally magnetic stones. Lodestone, however, is the only type of magnetite that shows north-south polarity. That means that the ends of a piece of lodestone will always point toward the Earth's magnetic north and south poles.

Figure 4.1   Iron nails will stick to a piece of lodestone.

Because these natural magnets pointed toward the planet's poles, people started to call the opposite ends of a magnet the north and south poles. As early as 1086, this north-south polarity also led to people using slivers of lodestone to help them find their way around. The ancient Chinese, for example, made early compasses to guide their ships by dangling slivers of lodestone from pieces of string. From there, the use of magnetic compasses spread to the Arabs who traded with the Chinese in the thirteenth century.

MAGNETIC DOMAINS

Some materials, such as iron, can easily be magnetized if rubbed by another magnet. However, iron can also be easily demagnetized. Therefore, iron magnets are called temporary magnets. Steel, on the other hand, is much harder to magnetize, but this makes it much harder to demagnetize, too. Therefore, steel can be used to make permanent magnets.

Iron and other elements that can be used to make magnets exhibit a unique property at the atomic level when they are exposed to a magnet—the electrons in groups of atoms line up parallel with each other in regions called magnetic domains. In other words, in each domain, the electrons are lined up in the same direction. However, in order for a metal to be magnetized, all of its magnetic domains must be lined up, too. Only when all the magnetic domains and the electrons in those domains are lined up in the same direction will a metal become a magnet.

Lodestone and iron are not the only naturally magnetic materials. Cobalt, nickel, steel (which contains iron), and some of the rare earth metals such as gadolinium and dysprosium, are magnetic, too. However, only iron, steel, nickel, cobalt, and gadolinium can be turned into permanent magnets at room temperature. Dysprosium requires low temperatures in order to get its domains lined up correctly. These materials are called **ferromagnetic** materials. Ferromagnetism gets its name from iron (the Latin word for "iron" is *ferrum*). Regardless of the fact that the other four elements do not have iron in them, they are still called ferromagnetic materials. In fact, any metal that is strongly attracted to a magnet is a ferromagnetic material.

How Did It Get Its Name?

While it is known that the word *electricity* comes from the Greek word meaning "amber," no one really knows the origin of the word *magnet*. Many sources say that the word comes from Magnesia, an area in ancient Asia Minor where large deposits of lodestone can be found. Other explanations include the story of a shepherd named Magnes who found the nails of his shoes or the metal tip of his staff (depending on which legend you read) being attracted to lodestone. However it got its name, magnetism is still a powerful force.

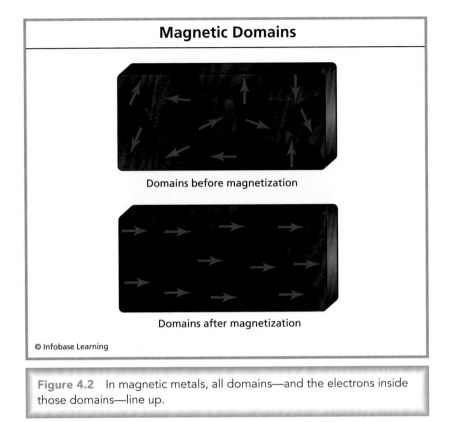

Magnetic Domains

Domains before magnetization

Domains after magnetization

© Infobase Learning

Figure 4.2 In magnetic metals, all domains—and the electrons inside those domains—line up.

The magnetic domains in a temporary magnet can be easily rearranged. An iron nail that has been magnetized can be demagnetized by hitting or dropping it, for example. When the domains go back to their random orientations, the nail will no longer be magnetized.

Sometimes a permanent magnet can be demagnetized, too. This usually happens when the magnet is heated. Heating causes the atoms inside the magnet to move rapidly in random directions. This random movement causes the magnetic domains to become disordered and the material will no longer be magnetized. So *permanent* does not always mean permanent.

MAGNETIC POLES

Every magnet has a north pole and a south pole. If a bar magnet is cut in half, the magnetic domains will align themselves in such a way to create a new north or south pole. The magnet can be cut into smaller and smaller pieces, but, in the end, it will still have a north and a south pole.

Like charges, scientists soon discovered that opposite poles (north-south) attract each other while like poles (north-north or south-south) repel. In 1785, Charles Coulomb used his torsion balance to find out how much attractive or repulsive force magnets exerted on each other. Like charges, Coulomb found that it depended on the size of the magnet (the larger the magnet, the larger the force) and the distance between the poles (the closer they were together, the larger the force). Also, like charges, the poles of a magnet are surrounded by a field—a magnetic field.

Making a Magnet

There are essentially three types of magnets—permanent magnets, temporary magnets, and electromagnets. Magnetite is a natural permanent magnet. Bar magnets are also permanent magnets. Permanent magnets retain their magnetic properties all the time.

A temporary magnet, on the other hand, is a piece of metal (usually iron) that can be temporarily magnetized. Temporary magnets are easy to make. To make your own magnet, you need a piece of iron, such as an iron nail, a permanent magnet (a bar magnet, for example), and a few paper clips (to prove that you have magnetized the iron nail).

Before magnetizing the iron nail, try bringing it close to the paper clips. Most likely, nothing will happen. To make the iron nail pick up the paper clips, you have to magnetize it by lining up its magnetic domains so that they are all pointing in the same direction. To do this, rub the bar magnet in one direction along the nail (for example, from the head of the nail to the point or from the point to the head). Do not change the direction you rub the bar magnet over the nail. Continue to rub the bar magnet in the same direction until the nail picks up the paper clips. By doing this, you will create a temporary magnet.

Magnetic Poles

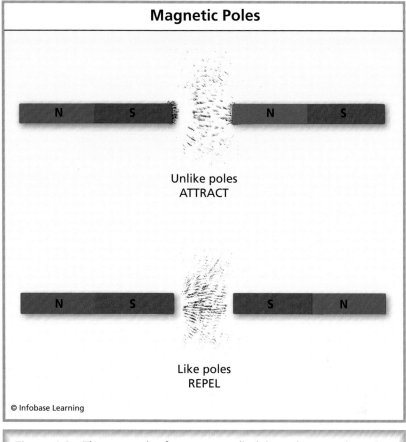

Unlike poles
ATTRACT

Like poles
REPEL

© Infobase Learning

Figure 4.3 The two ends of a magnet, called the poles, are where the greatest concentration of force is.

MAGNETIC FIELDS

Just as electric field lines always move in the same direction (from the positive charge toward the negative charge), so do magnetic field lines. Magnetic field lines are always drawn from the north pole toward the south pole. You can see the magnetic field lines produced by a permanent magnet by placing iron filings on a piece of paper and the magnet below the paper. The iron filings will arrange themselves with the magnetic field lines that surround the magnet.

Like an electric field, a magnetic field is an invisible force that has power and can do work. Magnetism is the physical effect of a

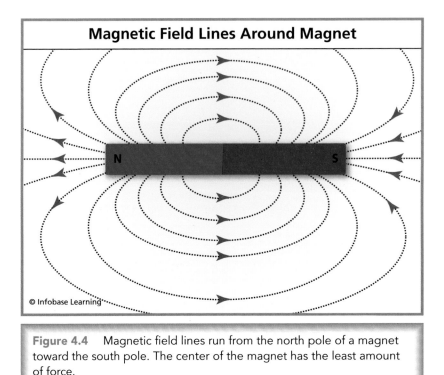

Figure 4.4 Magnetic field lines run from the north pole of a magnet toward the south pole. The center of the magnet has the least amount of force.

magnetic field. Even though you cannot feel it, you are surrounded by magnetic fields all the time. Planet Earth itself, in fact, is one big magnet.

EARTH'S MAGNETISM

People had been using compasses to find their way from one place to another for centuries before someone came along and explained how they might work. That someone was William Gilbert (1544–1603), Queen Elizabeth's doctor. Gilbert used a perfectly round chunk of lodestone to represent the Earth. Using this model magnetic Earth, Gilbert was able to show that the Earth's own magnetic properties were responsible for the north-south orientation of compass needles. In 1600, Gilbert wrote a book (called *The Magnet*) explaining his belief that the Earth was a gigantic magnet. Gilbert showed that, basically, the planet works as if it has a huge bar magnet at its core.

Before Gilbert's experiments and explanations, people commonly believed that either Polaris (also called the North Star or the Pole Star) or a magnetic island sitting at the North Pole caused compass needles to swing northward.

Today, scientists believe that the magnetic field surrounding Earth is not the result of its solid iron core. Instead, it is believed that Earth's magnetic field is produced by moving ionized particles of iron in Earth's liquid outer core.

Earth's magnetic poles, however, do not line up exactly with its geographic poles. Earth's rotational axis passes through the geographic North and South poles. In the northern hemisphere, geographic north points toward (or very close to) Polaris (explaining the ancient belief that Polaris attracted the north-seeking compass needle). Geographic north is sometimes called "true north," too. True north is the north that is shown on maps. If an imaginary line were passed through the magnetic north and south poles of Earth, the line would be tilted approximately 12° from the North and South Poles (the rotational axis of Earth). Because of this tilt and the way the magnetic field lines are shaped around Earth, compasses in most places on Earth do not point to geographic north.

The difference (in degrees) between magnetic north and geographic north at a particular location is called the magnetic declination. The magnetic declination for some areas can be quite high. For example, in some parts of Alaska, compasses point as much as 30° east of geographic north. This declination must be taken into

The World's Strongest Magnet

Magnetic field strength is measured in teslas, which are named for Nikola Tesla (1856–1943), the man who invented alternating current (AC). The most powerful magnet in the world has a magnetic field of 45 tesla. (For comparison, Earth's magnetic field is one-twenty-thousandths of a tesla.) This magnet weighs 35 tons (31.7 metric tons) and is housed at the National High Magnetic Field Laboratory in Tallahassee, Florida.

account when navigating with a compass and a map. To make matters more interesting, Earth's magnetic poles do not always stay in the same position. They move around. In fact, magnetic north today is not in the same place it was 20 years ago, and most compasses will not point in the same direction they did 20 years ago, either. Companies that publish navigational maps must occasionally update them to take into account Earth's changing magnetic field.

About 750,000 years ago, the planet's poles switched places completely. This reversal in Earth's magnetic field has happened hundreds of times in the planet's history. According to geologic records, reversals occur, on average, about every 250,000 years. In the last 150 years, Earth's magnetic field has decreased by about 10%. Some scientists believe that this is setting the planet up for another magnetic field reversal. These scientists believe that the reversal of the North Pole and South Pole could happen at any time—with unknown consequences.

Earth's magnetic south pole is near its geographic North Pole. Because opposite poles of magnets are attracted to each other, the

Finding True North

If you want to know what the magnetic declination is in your particular location, all you need is a piece of paper, two pencils, a compass, and a protractor. At exactly noon on a sunny day, go outside and hold one pencil perpendicular to the ground. The shadow of the pencil will point to geographic north. Mark down the direction of the pencil's shadow on the piece of paper. Now, check the compass and indicate the direction of magnetic north on the same piece of paper. Measure the angle between the two lines with a protractor and you will have the difference between geographic and magnetic north at your location. This difference between geographic north and magnetic north causes compasses in the northeastern part of the United States to point north-northwest. A compass on the west coast of the United States, on the other hand, would point north-northeast.

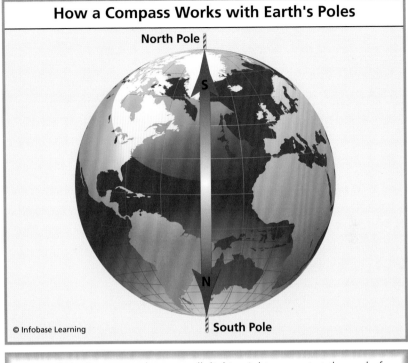

How a Compass Works with Earth's Poles

North Pole

South Pole

© Infobase Learning

Figure 4.5 A compass has a small, lightweight magnet at the end of a needle, balancing freely on a pivot point. This enables the compass to pick up the slight force of the magnetic field within Earth.

north pole of a compass will seek the south magnetic pole of Earth. This attraction causes the compass needle to swing so that it points toward the north. Likewise, Earth's magnetic north pole is near its geographic South Pole. Therefore, a compass's south pole is attracted to this pole.

As useful as compasses are for navigation, there is an even more important advantage that Earth's magnetic field provides humans. It protects us from the high-energy charged particles given off by the Sun. This stream of charged particles is called solar wind. The solar wind blasts away from the Sun at 894,775 miles per hour (nearly 400 kilometers per second). High-energy, fast moving particles like those in the solar wind could do great harm to living things. Luckily for us, Earth's magnetic field, which stretches about 36,000 miles (58,000 km) out into space, deflects most of these particles away from the planet—and away from us.

Migration and the Earth's Magnetism

Some birds (and butterflies) travel thousands of miles every year in their annual migration. How do they find their way back to the same places year after year? Scientists believe that birds may have a built-in compass that can sense the Earth's magnetic field lines. Scientists have found that pigeons, for example, actually have traces of ferromagnetic metal in their skulls. Some types of bacteria also have ferromagnetic metals that help them swim along magnetic field lines. Scientists believe that whales may possess the same mechanism for finding their way from their feeding grounds to their mating areas all around the globe.

In the process of deflecting the solar wind, Earth's magnetic field puts on a little light show for us, too. The charged particles coming from the Sun cause the colors, lights, and movement of the aurora borealis, which is also called the Northern Lights. Scientists have discovered that as Earth's magnetic field lines store energy from the solar wind that bombards them, they get pulled away from the surface of Earth and stretch out like rubber bands. Just like a rubber band that has been stretched too far, these magnetic field lines eventually snap. The energy that is released when the magnetic field lines snap throws charged particles back toward Earth where the field lines reconnect. The movement, or "dancing," of the Northern Lights is caused by these magnetic storms. These storms can also disrupt the global positioning system (GPS) and communication signals on Earth by knocking satellites out of their proper orbits. They can also cause power outages. Scientists are hoping that studying the Northern Lights will help them understand these magnetic storms better and, one day, allow them to solve the communication problems they cause.

Electromagnetism

Electricity and magnetism have existed in the natural world since the beginning of time, but it was not until the nineteenth century that scientists figured out how they were related and what they could really do. It took a little while longer to actually harness the two and make them do the work of lighting our homes, cooling our food, and allowing us to surf the Internet.

DISCOVERING ELECTROMAGNETISM

In July 1820, a Danish physicist named Hans Christian Ørsted (also spelled Orstead) (1777–1851), was the first person to describe the relationship between electricity and magnetism. During a lecture at the University of Copenhagen, Ørsted showed that if he brought a compass close to a wire that was carrying an electric current, the compass needle would point toward the wire instead of toward magnetic north. If he changed the direction of the current, the compass needle would point in the opposite direction, away from the wire.

When the current stopped moving through the wire, the compass needle would return to magnetic north. This action proved that the wire itself did not have magnetic properties. In fact, Ørsted was using copper wire. Copper is a nonmagnetic metal. If the wire itself was not causing the compass needle to move, Ørsted reasoned that an electrical wire with current flowing though it must be surrounded by a magnetic field. In other words, Ørsted discovered that a magnetic field could be caused by moving charges.

Ørsted soon discovered that the larger the wire he used to carry the current (remember that larger wires can carry more current), the larger the magnetic field he would produce. He also found that the strength of the magnetic field decreased the further away you moved from the current-carrying wire. In time, Ørsted determined that wires were not needed at all. Electrons moving through a vacuum tube (using no wires), for example, would cause a magnet to orient itself perpendicular to the tube (the flow, or current, of electrons), too.

André-Marie Ampère (1775–1836), a French physicist, found out about Ørsted's discovery and did some experiments of his own. Ampère found that when he placed two wires side by side with current flowing though them and traveling in the same direction, the wires were attracted to each other. Yet when he switched the current in one wire so that the currents ran in opposite directions, the wires repelled each other.

Ampère also discovered that wrapping a wire in a spiral generated a stronger magnetic field. As the current went though each loop of the coiled wire, more current passed through a smaller space and,

Doorbells

Solenoids are useful in many devices around the home. One of the simplest devices to rely on a solenoid is the doorbell. When someone at the front door pushes the doorbell button, it switches on a current in the doorbell circuit. When the current is turned on, the metal rod at the core of the doorbell's solenoid is pulled back and strikes the chimes that make the doorbell "ring." When the person releases the doorbell button, the metal rod goes back to its original position, waiting for the next person to switch the current on.

Figure 5.1 A large electromagnet is used to lift waste iron and steel at a scrapyard.

as Ørsted found out, a larger current created a stronger magnetic field. Ampère called this coil of wire a **solenoid**.

William Sturgeon (1783–1850), an English physicist, produced the first **electromagnet**. He noticed that if an iron bar was placed inside the spiral of wire, it made the solenoid magnet stronger. In fact, the magnetic field generated by a solenoid can be made hundreds or even thousands of times stronger by putting a bar magnet in the middle of the coiled wire.

By 1827, American teacher and amateur physicist Joseph Henry (1797–1878) had reproduced Sturgeon's experiments and made an electromagnet that could lift 9 pounds (4 kilograms). He soon discovered that he could make an even stronger electromagnet by coiling more wire around the magnet. And he found that he could wrap more coils if he used insulated wire to make the spiral. By 1832, Henry was able to make an electromagnet that could lift 3,000 pounds (1,360 kg) using this method.

Henry had a lot of fun lifting heavy objects, such as blacksmith anvils. He would allow an electric current to flow through a wire, which, in turn, activated the electromagnet. After attaching several anvils to his electromagnet, Henry would lift the whole collection up into the sky using scaffolding. Once he was satisfied that the anvils were high enough, Henry turned off the electricity flowing through the wire. With the electromagnet turned off, the heavy anvils came crashing down. "This never fails to produce a great sensation," wrote Henry.

Henry did not stop at just scaring the villagers and amusing himself with electromagnets, though. He also discovered the basic principles of the telegraph. He did this by lengthening the wire that led from the battery to the electromagnet. When he connected the battery to the wire, electric current flowed through the wire and powered up the electromagnet, even if the electromagnet was far away from the battery. He put a small metal tab (that looked like a small, clickable castanet) near the electromagnet. When the electromagnet came on, the metal tab was pulled toward the electromagnet and produced an audible click. When the electromagnet was turned off, the metal tab popped back to its original shape, again producing a click. Henry eventually gave up teaching and went on to become one of America's greatest physicists and the director of the Smithsonian Institution.

ELECTROMAGNETIC INDUCTION

About the same time Henry was doing his experiments, Michael Faraday also became interested in Ørsted's discovery. Knowing that an

Making an Electromagnet

You can make an electromagnet yourself by wrapping thin, plastic-coated wire around an iron nail. Wrap the wire tightly around the nail from the head of the nail to almost the point. Press the coils of wire as close together as you can. The more wraps of the wire you can get onto the nail, the stronger your magnet will be. Using the side of a pair of open scissors, carefully strip the plastic coating off of the ends of the wire. Hook the two ends of the wire to the terminals of a 9-volt battery. You may have to use a couple of pieces of tape to keep the ends in place. When the ends of the wire are attached to the battery terminals, the electricity flowing through the wire aligns the magnetic domains in the iron nail. To test your electromagnet, use the point of the nail to see how many paper clips you can pick up.

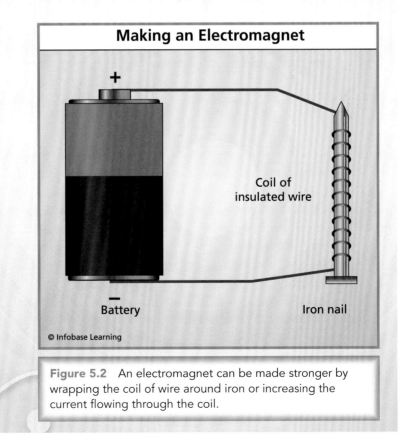

Making an Electromagnet

+

Coil of insulated wire

Battery

Iron nail

© Infobase Learning

Figure 5.2 An electromagnet can be made stronger by wrapping the coil of wire around iron or increasing the current flowing through the coil.

electric current could produce a magnetic field, Faraday wondered if a magnetic field could produce electricity. He found that, indeed, it could. However, it was not just the existence of a magnetic field, but rather the movement of the field that created a current. Faraday discovered that if he pushed a magnet into a coil of wire, a current would flow in one direction though the wire. The current would flow the opposite way when the magnet was pulled out of the coil. When Faraday stopped moving the magnet, the electric current stopped, too. If he started moving the magnet again, the electric current re-appeared. This phenomenon is called **electromagnetic induction**. Therefore, Faraday surmised, to produce an electric current the magnet must be moving. A stationary magnet will do nothing. He deduced that something in the magnet was traveling from the magnet to the wire. Scientists now call that something a magnetic field.

Faraday went on to show that the strength of the current that was induced depended on how strong the magnet was (stronger magnets produced more current), how fast the magnet was moving (moving the magnet faster produced more current), and the number of turns in the wire (more turns equaled more current). Together, Faraday's and Henry's discoveries made commercial production of electricity possible.

Junkyard Cranes

Electromagnets can be made strong enough to lift many tons. One area where electromagnets are used is in the cranes used by junkyards to place junked cars into a crusher. The crane operator works the crane by controlling the current that moves though a solenoid. When the current is switched on, the magnet comes to life and picks up a car. Keeping the current flowing, the crane operator moves the car into position over the crusher. Once the car is in position, the operator turns off the current in the coil, which switches off the magnet. Because the car is no longer attracted to the magnet, it falls into the crusher and is soon crushed into a compact piece of scrap metal that can be shipped somewhere else to serve some other purpose.

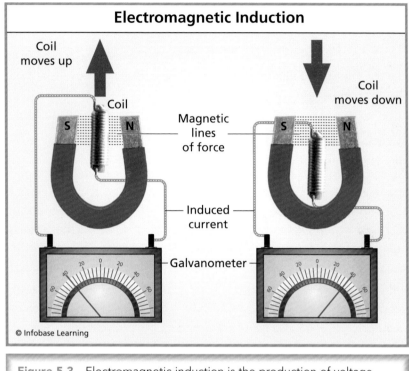

Electromagnetic Induction

Coil moves up

Coil

S   N

Magnetic lines of force

Coil moves down

S   N

Induced current

Galvanometer

© Infobase Learning

Figure 5.3   Electromagnetic induction is the production of voltage across a conductor—usually a piece of wire—moving across a magnetic field.

ELECTROMAGNETIC THEORY

By the end of the eighteenth century, scientists knew four major facts about electricity and magnetism. James Clerk Maxwell (1831–1879) put these facts together and outlined what physicists today call the electromagnetic theory:

- An electric charge is surrounded by an electric field. Like charges repel and opposite charges attract.
- Magnetic poles always exist in pairs. In other words, a north pole cannot exist without a south pole. Like poles repel and opposite poles attract.
- A moving charge, or a changing electric field, can produce a magnetic field.

 • A moving magnet, or a changing magnetic field, can produce an electric field.

Most of the electronics and machinery that we use today, from electric motors to electrical power plants, would not exist without the electromagnetic theory.

ELECTRIC MOTORS

An electric motor is a device that converts electrical energy into mechanical energy. To make a simple electric motor, a coil of wire is suspended between two permanent magnets. The two magnets are arranged on opposite ends of the coil of wire. One magnet's north pole is pointed toward one end of the coil of wire while the other magnet's south pole is pointed in the direction of the other end of the coil. This situation creates a magnetic field between the two poles of the magnets where the wire coil is suspended.

Spinning Electrons

If moving charges can create a magnetic field and electrons move around an atom's nucleus, it would seem as if each electron would create its own magnetic field. If this were true, then every material made of atoms (which is everything) should be at least slightly magnetic. In fact, electrons do produce their own magnetic field. However, because there are usually several electrons moving around an atom at once and each electron has a random movement, the magnetic fields of the electrons cancel each other out, leaving the atom with a net zero magnetic field.

However, electrons also spin. This spin creates a magnetic field, too. In most materials, electrons with opposite spins pair up, canceling their magnetic fields. However, in iron and a few other materials, the magnetic field of the spinning electrons is not entirely cancelled out, leaving the atoms with a net magnetic field. This spinning of the electrons is what causes the magnetic field seen in a permanent magnet.

To understand how an electric motor works, imagine the simplest coil of wire, one with only one loop. This loop is suspended in the magnetic field created between the two opposite poles of the magnets. This loop of wire must spin in order for the motor to do its job. Because the coil of wire needs to spin in an electric motor, it cannot be attached with fixed wires. If it was, the wires would get so twisted that friction would eventually stop the motion of the coil and the motor would no longer work. Instead, the current is supplied through a device called a commutator. Commutators are usually split rings or cylinders that touch contacts (which are called brushes). The brushes are attached to a source of current (such as a battery). One brush is attached to the positive battery terminal and the other is attached to the negative one. Current flows through the brushes, though the commutator, and into the coil of wire. After every half turn of the coil, the current in the coil reverses. When the current reverses, the magnetic field around the coil of wire also reverses. This reversal of the magnetic field keeps the coil rotating. The spinning coil of wire builds up kinetic energy (the energy of motion) and, therefore, electrical energy is converted into mechanical energy. The mechanical energy can be used to do work.

Newer, computer-controlled electric motors use a different method to keep the motor spinning. These new motors rely on

Right-hand Rule

The magnetic field lines produced by an electric current moving through a wire move in a circle around the wire in a particular direction. If the current is reversed, the magnetic field lines still move in a circle around the wire, but the direction of the magnetic field lines is reversed. Physicists use a method called the right-hand rule to help them determine the direction the magnetic field lines travel around a current-carrying wire. To use the right-hand rule, point the thumb of your right hand in the direction the current is flowing through a wire. Curl the fingers of your right hand toward your palm. The direction of your curled fingers is the direction of the magnetic field lines.

computers instead of commutators. To visualize how these new motors work, imagine a metal clock hand pointing to the twelve o'clock position. This imaginary clock has two electromagnets—one at the three o'clock position and one at the nine o'clock position. If the electromagnet at three o'clock is turned on, the clock hand will move toward the three o'clock position. If the electromagnet stays on, the hand would stop at three o'clock. Yet if the electromagnet is turned off before the clock hand reaches that position, the hand's momentum will make it keep moving. This momentum would cause the hand to overshoot the three o'clock position. If the other electromagnet, the one at the nine o'clock position, is then turned on, the clock hand would continue to move around the clock face pulled by the electromagnet at nine o'clock. If the electromagnet is turned off just as the hand reaches the nine o'clock position, its momentum would again cause the hand to swing past the nine o'clock position. If the three o'clock electromagnet is then turned on again, the hand continues to move round and round the clock face. This is, basically, what happens in these new electric motors, too. A computer turns the electromagnets on and off at set intervals, causing the motor to spin continuously.

ELECTRIC GENERATORS

Electric generators serve a function opposite that of an electric motor. Generators convert mechanical energy into electrical energy. This electrical energy can be in the form of either direct or alternating current, depending on the type of generator. Generators have the same parts that electric motors have—a coil of wire, a magnetic field the wire can rotate in, and a way to reverse the current in the coil of wire (a commutator).

In fact, depending on the desired use, an electric motor can sometimes be adjusted to function as a generator and an electric generator could function as a motor. If an outside source of current is supplied to the device, the coil turns and it acts as a motor. However, if the coil is mechanically turned, the movement of the coil through the magnetic field induces a current that can be collected. Therefore, the same device can also act as a generator.

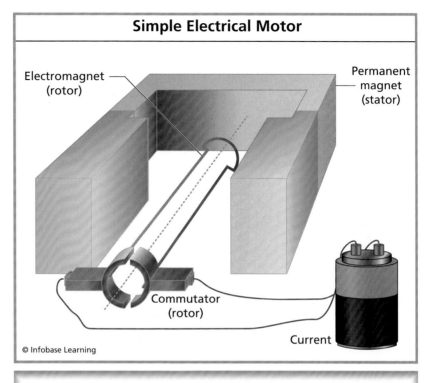

Simple Electrical Motor

Electromagnet (rotor)

Permanent magnet (stator)

Commutator (rotor)

Current

© Infobase Learning

Figure 5.4 The simplest type of electric motor has two main parts. On the outside is a permanent horseshoe magnet called the stator. Between the poles of the stator is a loop of wire through which electric current flows. This is called the rotor. When electricity flows through the rotor, it becomes an electromagnet. The poles of the rotor interact with the poles of the stator, making the motor turn. In order to keep the motor spinning, a device called a commutator changes the direction of current flow in the rotor every half turn. This way, the similar poles of the two magnets are always near each other and they repel, which makes the motor turn.

Some electric vehicles, for example, use their brakes to generate more power to keep running. During acceleration and driving, electric cars use electricity from the battery to move the wheels of the car. However, during braking, the car's electronic controller cuts off the electricity to the motor. The kinetic energy (energy of motion) of the car's wheels is then used to mechanically turn the motor and generate electricity that can help charge the car's battery. This process is called regenerative braking. Unlike standard friction braking systems, regenerative braking systems use the car's kinetic energy to produce more power instead of converting the kinetic energy into wasted heat.

Mechanically turning the coils in a generator can be done in several different ways. Water, collected by dams, for example, can turn turbines that, in turn, induce a current. Windmills harness the power of the wind by turning the windmill's blades to induce a current. In fact, just about any type of motion can be converted into electrical energy. The challenge is to do it efficiently and in a cost-effective enough manner for it to be useful.

Modern Life: Electricity and Electromagnets

M any of the appliances and electronic devices that we use every day contain electric motors. Even those devices that do not have motors, however, often use electricity, electromagnetism, or a combination of both in order to do their jobs.

THE TELEGRAPH

Joseph Henry may have figured out the basics of the telegraph in 1831, but it was not until Samuel Morse (1791–1872) built on Henry's original idea in 1844 that the first large, commercial working telegraph linking Washington and Baltimore was built. The invention of the telegraph changed the way information was spread.

Before the telegraph, it took a long time for mail to get from one place to another in the United States. With the invention of a practical telegraph, however, important information, like financial news, could be relayed in just seconds instead of days or weeks. Suddenly, a company with employees in New York and San Francisco could be in instant contact with one another. This changed the way companies did business.

People not only needed to get news across the country, they also needed a faster way to get news from around the world. Why would this be so important? Well, take for example, the Battle of New Orleans. This was a battle that was fought during the War of 1812. Many soldiers died in what was the worst battle of the entire war. This is, of course, tragic in and of itself, but the real tragedy is that the battle should never have been fought in the first place. The Battle of New Orleans took place on January 8, 1815. Yet a treaty to end the war was signed in Ghent, Belgium, on December 24, 1814—more than two weeks earlier! The war was over, but the men who fought and died in the Battle of New Orleans had no way of knowing that because, at the time, it took messages from Europe at least 10 to 14 days to reach the United States. In 1866, two decades after the first telegraph cable linked Washington and Baltimore and more than 50 years after the Battle of New Orleans was fought, the first working transatlantic telegraph cable was laid across the ocean floor. The speed with which information could now get from one place to another changed the world forever. It not only changed the way businesses did business and the way wars were fought, it also had other effects on people as well—such as creating the need for synchronized clocks.

THE TELEPHONE

The next big leap forward in communication came along in 1876 when Alexander Graham Bell (1847–1922) spoke into a telephone in one room and Thomas Watson (1854–1934), his assistant, heard Bell's voice speak the words, "Watson, come here. I want to see you," through the phone in the next room. By the time Watson heard those fateful words, the dot-and-dash system of Morse code and the telegraph had been around for about 30 years. And while the telegraph was a great step forward in communication, it was limited to transmitting only one message at a time. Bell hoped to make a system that could send and receive multiple messages over the same wire at the same time.

Bell developed the idea of the telephone while living in Boston. He was making a living as a tutor for the deaf when he met Mabel Hubbard, one of his students, and fell in love with her. However,

Mabel's parents were against a courtship between the young couple. Bell decided that if he could perfect an invention he'd been thinking about—the telephone—Mabel's parents might be swayed by the money and fame that came along with it and allow him to marry their daughter.

While Bell might have been motivated by his love for Mabel to perfect the telephone, this was not some random idea for making money that had popped into his head. Bell already had a lot of training and knowledge to help him in his quest. In fact, he came from a long line of men who studied the human voice and the creation of speech. His grandfather was an actor and an expert in elocution (which refers to the use of the voice in public speaking). Bell's father also spent his lifetime studying how people produced certain sounds because, like Mabel, Bell's mother was deaf. His father studied the mechanics of speech in an effort to help his wife communicate better. He also taught his sons to communicate with their mother. As young men, Alexander and his brother even made an artificial throat and lips using the larynx of a dead sheep and bellows. The bellows served as the air source (the lungs, so to speak). By manipulating their homemade tongue and lips, the boys were able to make the sheep's voice box bleat out "Mama!"

Before coming up with the idea of the telephone, Bell did extensive research on telegraphs. From this research, he knew that electricity would flow down a wire in a steady current from the battery to which it was connected. He also knew that if the wire was twisted or bent, the electricity did not flow as well. This is because a bent or twisted wire provided resistance to the flow of electrons (like a narrowed water pipe would provide resistance to the flow of water).

Bell found that if he put a piece of parchment paper up to his lips when he spoke, the vibrations of his speech would be transferred to the piece of paper. If he placed the other side of the piece of paper against a wire, each puff of breath that he released when he spoke caused the parchment paper to vibrate against the wire. This caused the wire to bend slightly. When he stopped speaking, the wire was no longer bent and the electricity flowed freely though the wire again. This fluctuating resistance would be the basis for Bell's invention.

Bell's gamble to impress Mabel's parents with his invention paid off. They encouraged the 28-year-old Bell to apply for a patent for his new invention. He did so, and it was only hours before another inventor,

Elisha Gray (1835–1901), who independently invented his own version of the telephone, reached the patent office. Mabel's parents gave permission for Bell and Mabel to get married not long afterward.

Needless to say, William Orton, who was the head of Western Union, the world's largest telegraph company at the time, was not at all happy with Bell's success. What could the businessman do about it? The first action he took was to hire Thomas Edison (1847–1931) and Elisha Gray, two of the top inventors of the time. Orton asked the two men to drive Bell's fledgling company, Bell Telephone, out of business by developing an even superior telephone. Edison agreed to try.

Edison saw a flaw in Bell's design on which he thought he could capitalize. In Bell's design, vibrations of the human voice were needed to start an electric signal traveling down the phone wire. The problem with this method was that the signal became too weak after only a few hundred yards or so. To get the signal to travel further than that, the speaker had to yell. Edison realized, however, that if a strong electric current was flowing though the telephone wire even before a person started speaking, all the vibrations picked up by the microphone would have to do is modify that signal, not generate it. This prevented the signal from fading away, so telephone messages could be sent over a distance of several miles.

This is still the basic concept of how a telephone works today. When you speak into a telephone, you speak into a microphone. Sound waves produced when you speak cause the microphone to vibrate. Depending on the type of sound you are making, these vibrations are different. If you emit a high-pitched squeal into the microphone, for example, it will vibrate rapidly. It hardly vibrates at all when you are silent, however. These vibrations cause a thin piece of plastic or metal (the modern version of Bell's parchment) to vibrate against a wire carrying a current. When the plastic or metal foil presses on the wire, it is bent and the resistance is changed. Remember that according to Ohm's law, resistance, current, and voltage are all related. Therefore, a change in resistance will also cause a change in voltage. The pattern of your speech can be duplicated exactly by the differing voltages conducted down the phone wire.

On the other end of the telephone, is a receiver. An electromagnet in the receiver produces a varying magnetic field in response to this changing voltage. The varying magnetic field causes a thin metal

Figure 6.1 Thomas Edison exhibits a replica of his first successful incandescent lamp, which gave 16 candlepower of illumination, in contrast to the ultimate in today's achievement: a 50,000 watt, or 150,000 candlepower, lamp.

diaphragm to vibrate and produce sound waves. The sound waves hit your ear drum with the same intensity and frequency as the sound waves produced by the speaker, allowing you to hear what was said.

In the end, Edison did help modify and perfect Bell's idea of the telephone, but he failed to put Bell Telephone out of business. In fact, today, Bell Telephone is still operating, but now under the name of AT&T.

THE LIGHT BULB

Thomas Edison did not stop experimenting and researching, however. He continued to think about other ways different resistances in different parts of an electric wire could be utilized. He turned his

Television

Before the widespread availability of plasma television screens, most television sets were made with cathode ray tubes (CRTs). Until recently, most computer screens used CRTs, too. A CRT produces a beam of electrons. The front of the tube is coated in a special chemical called a phosphor. The chemical lights up when the beam of electrons hit the molecules in the phosphor. Electromagnets are used to tug the beam of electrons back and forth across the tube. As the electron beam moves, it hits red, green, or blue phosphors, creating the picture. The electromagnets are driven by the signals put out by television broadcasting stations. Newer displays, such as plasma flat panel televisions and liquid crystal display (LCD) computer monitors, contain a different technology.

Figure 6.2 Old-fashioned TVs, like this one cut in half, use a cathode-ray tube to get images on screen. The tube fires a single beam of electrons across the screen very quickly. The electrons hit tiny pixels one after the other, making them each glow in turn. It all happens so quickly that you don't notice the flickering—just the TV's images.

interest to electric lighting. He knew that if certain metals were heated up enough, they would glow white-hot and give off light. He had also heard stories of Aleksandr Lodygin (1847–1923), a Russian inventor who, in 1872, lit up the Admiralty Dockyards in St. Petersburg, Russia, with 200 electric lights. The problem with Lodygin's lamps was that they burned out in just a few hours because so much power was passing through them that their filaments melted quickly.

To prevent this problem, Edison experimented with different metals. Because platinum had the highest melting point of any metal known at that time, Edison wanted to use platinum filaments in his electric lights. However, platinum was very expensive. He also tried using nickel, but, like Lodygin's lamps, this bulb burned out too fast. Unable to find an inexpensive enough metal, Edison tried plant material instead. He tested paper, cotton, and cork. However, none of these substances worked very well. Eventually, some of Edison's assistants found a plant in Japan, the Madake bamboo plant, which worked better than any filament material they had tried so far. Using Madake bamboo as a filament in his light bulb, Edison succeeded in making a bulb that could burn for more than 1,500 hours. He also discovered that if all of the oxygen from inside the light bulb was removed, the filament would not burn as quickly and would, therefore, last even longer. Today, the filament of most incandescent (a material so hot that it gives off light and heat) light bulbs is made from the element tungsten, and they are filled with a nonreactive gas like argon, a noble gas.

Along with light bulbs that lasted longer, Edison and his team of scientists also developed the screw tops that bulbs still have today and the screw-in sockets that they fit into. The inventors got their inspiration from the screw-tops of kerosene cans. (On a side note, light bulbs got their name because people thought that the glass containers that Edison used looked like tulip bulbs.)

SEMICONDUCTORS

In the 1920s and 1930s, most electrical specialists still believed that all substances could be broken down into two categories—those that always conducted electricity (conductors) and those that never did (insulators). Metals such as copper and steel were conductors. Glass and wood were not—end of discussion. Well, luckily for those of us that work or play on computers, the world is not quite that simple.

Silicon, an element that can be found in quartz and sand, is neither a conductor nor a nonconductor. It can be either of these things at different times and under different circumstances. In the early 1940s, radio technicians were the first to discover that silicon could act as a perfect insulator and prevent the passage of a current of electrons. However, silicon did not always act this way. At other times, it could pick up a stream of electrons and allow them to flow through it. In other words, it acted as a conductor. Indeed, silicon was a new kind of substance—a **semiconductor**. Semiconductors have properties in between conductors and insulators. Scientists later found other elements, such as germanium, that could act as a semiconductor, too.

By the late 1940s, scientists began to unravel exactly what was happening inside silicon that made it act this way. Sometimes, silicon forms crystals that are in a perfect shape that is called a lattice. When silicon is in this lattice structure, none of its electrons are free to move around. With no free electrons, the silicon acts as an insulator. Therefore, very little electricity can get through a silicon crystal when it is in its pure, perfect lattice structure.

The silicon that is found in nature is rarely found in its pure form. In fact, most silicon has tiny cracks or gaps in the lattice. Other elements, such as phosphorous, will often wedge themselves into those cracks. When phosphorous inhabits the cracks in the silicon, it brings its electrons along. These extra electrons inside the silicon lattice change the way the semiconductor behaves.

The process of adding small amounts of impurities, such as phosphorous, to a semiconductor in a laboratory is called doping. The impurities that are added are called dopants. There are two types of dopants—n-type and p-type. N-type dopants, like phosphorous, add free electrons to a semiconductor. These dopants are called n-type because they introduce excess negative charges into the semiconductor lattice. Because there are now extra electrons to move through the semiconductor, it acts as a conductor.

When silicon is in its pure form, each of its atoms has four valence electrons and bonds with four other silicon atoms. P-type dopants are chemicals that only have three valence electrons (n-type have five). Boron and gallium are examples of elements used as p-type dopants. Because boron, for example, has only three valence electrons, it can only bond with three silicon atoms. The absence of the fourth electron leaves a hole in the semiconductor's lattice structure. Electricity can be conducted through these holes as electrons from one atom move through the hole to another atom. Because holes are caused by an absence of electrons, they can be thought of as positive charges, giving the p-type dopants their name. Just a tiny amount of either n-type or p-type impurities can make silicon into a good electrical conductor.

TRANSISTORS

When an n-type semiconductor and a p-type semiconductor are put together into one device, you get a device that will let a current flow in one direction, but not in the other. This type of device is called a **diode**. Diodes are often used in electronic devices to protect the components inside the device in the event that you put its battery in backward.

In the late 1940s, two American scientists—Walter Brattain (1902–1987) and John Bardeen (1908–1991)—working for Bell Laboratories (part of the company started by Alexander Graham Bell) discovered that if they made a three-tiered alternating sandwich of doped silicon, they could make an atomic-level switch that could convert silicon from a conductor into an insulator. Basically, they had invented an atomic-level on/off switch.

Because this sandwich could open or close a circuit, or, in other words, it could transfer resistance, the scientists called it a *transistor*. There are two types of standard transistors—NPN transistors and PNP transistors. The letters refer to the type of dopants used in the layers and in which order they are stacked. Transistors look like two diodes sitting side by side. This arrangement should block the flow of current from both directions. And they do, unless the current is supplied to the middle layer of the transistor. When this is the case, electrons can flow through the semiconductor just fine. In fact, Brattain and Bardeen found that even a small current supplied to the middle layer of the transistor would make a much larger current flow through the three layers. This meant that the transistors could be used as amplifiers, and that even a weak electrical input could result in a larger output.

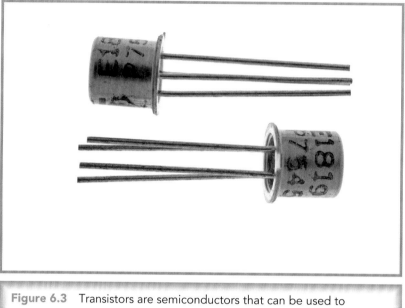

Figure 6.3 Transistors are semiconductors that can be used to increase and switch electronic signals.

Much of Brattain and Bardeen's research was funded by Bell Laboratories and they were one of the first companies to take advantage of the new, tiny transistors. Because Alexander Graham Bell's wife, Mabel, was deaf and Bardeen's wife was hard of hearing, the first product Bell Laboratories concentrated on making with these devices was a hearing aid. Hearing aids already existed in the late 1940s, but they were wired very much like telephones and were large and difficult to carry around (much less conceal). A transistor allowed for a much smaller battery to be used for hearing aids and made them much more practical and easy to use.

William Shockley (1910–1989) was a supervisor at Bell Laboratories when Brattain and Bardeen announced their discovery of transistors. Over the next several years, Shockley would improve on Brattain and Bardeen's original design. Transistors are probably one of the most important discoveries of the twentieth century. They are found in nearly all of the electronic devices we use today, including DVD players, computers, and cell phones. In 1956, Brattain, Bardeen, and Shockley won the Nobel Prize in physics for their discoveries.

Shockley eventually moved to a valley south of San Francisco—an area known today as Silicon Valley, where the headquarters of many large computer manufacturers have sprung up. Many young, talented engineers followed him there. One of those engineers, Robert Noyce (1927–1990), with the help of Jack Kilby (1923–2005), developed the technique of printing many transistors onto one computer chip (called an integrated circuit chip [IC] or microchip). An integrated chip is a miniature electronic circuit. With another young engineer, Gordon Moore (1929–), Noyce went on to cofound a company that could produce these chips in large quantities. Noyce and Moore named their company Intel.

Along with hearing aids, transistors also allowed radios to be built with much smaller batteries. The first transistor radios went on sale in the 1950s and suddenly, radios became portable. Computers would also be impossible without transistors. Millions of transistors can fit on an IC that can be held in the palm of your hand. The advances that allowed chips to get this small allow us to take along our computing power in the form of laptop computers, instead of having to rely on the room-sized colossal computers of decades past. Without the integrated circuit chip and silicon-based semiconductors, we would not have cell phones, ATMs, DVDs, or the Internet. This is because without semiconductors, many of the electronic devices we use every day would be much bigger, more expensive, and more energy consuming than they are now.

Electromagnetic Waves

What do your eyes, radios, televisions, and microwave ovens have in common? They are all very useful in everyday life and they all use electromagnetic waves. As you might imagine from their name, electromagnetic waves involve both electricity and magnetism.

JAMES CLERK MAXWELL

James Clerk Maxwell, the same man who outlined the electromagnetic theory, was also one of the first scientists to understand that electricity was made up of two parts—an electric part and a magnetic part. Maxwell realized that when electricity caused electrons to shake or ripple, the movement of the electrons changed the electric field surrounding them. And, as Maxwell stated in the electromagnetic theory, a changing electric field produces a magnetic field. As a magnetic field becomes stronger, changes in the magnetic field also produce an electric field. Therefore, as long as an electric current is supplied to start electrons moving, the changing electric field and changing magnetic field can sustain each other indefinitely. These alternating fields travel together through space as waves—electromagnetic waves, to be exact. The electric and magnetic fields that make up electromagnetic waves cannot exist separately.

Electromagnetic waves move very quickly. In fact, they all travel at the speed of light, which is approximately 186,000 miles per second (300 million meters per second). This speed would really be more accurately described as the speed of an electromagnetic wave. This measurement is called the speed of light because the speed of visible light waves was the first speed to be measured, but light is only one example of electromagnetic waves.

Electromagnetic waves can travel though matter. Visible light, for example, is an electromagnetic wave and it can travel through glass. X-rays are also electromagnetic waves and they can travel though a human body. However, unlike other types of waves, such as sound waves or waves of water, electromagnetic waves do not need to travel though matter. They can also travel through the vacuum of space.

To explain the phenomena of electromagnetic waves and how they work, Maxwell developed four complex mathematical formulas called Maxwell's equations. Maxwell's equations are still used by physicists today to define the behavior of electromagnetic fields. Without Maxwell's insight (and the work of future scientists who built upon his work), the wireless world that we live in today would not exist—and neither would televisions, radios, cell phones, GPS navigation systems, Bluetooth, or WiFi.

WAVELENGTH AND FREQUENCY

The wavelength of a wave is exactly what it sounds like—the length of the wave. It is the distance from the top, or crest, of the wave to the top of the next wave. Wavelength can also be measured from the bottom, or the trough, of one wave to the bottom of the next. In fact, technically, wavelength can be measured from any point on one wave to the same point on the next wave. Wave crests and troughs are just easy places to measure from. The wavelength of electromagnetic waves range from about the size of a proton (0.00000000000004 inch); (10^{-15} m), all the way up to about 2,485 miles (4,000 km) for some radio waves.

Frequency refers to how often an event happens. In the case of an electromagnetic wave, it means the number of waves that pass a particular spot every second. The more waves that pass that spot the higher the frequency. Waves with high frequencies have shorter wavelengths than those that have lower frequencies.

Frequencies are measured in hertz. One hertz is equal to one wave per second. The shortest of the electromagnetic waves (10^{-15} m) has a frequency of 10^{23} Hz. The longest radio wave's frequency is about 76 Hz. Electromagnetic waves are classified according to their frequencies. In order, from lowest to highest frequency, are radio waves, microwaves, infrared radiation, visible light, ultraviolet radiation, X-rays, and gamma rays. Together, these waves make up the electromagnetic spectrum.

RADIO WAVES

Radio waves have the lowest frequencies and longest wavelengths of all of the electromagnetic waves on the electromagnetic spectrum. Depending on the frequency wanted, radio waves can be made by various types of transmitters. A transmitter is an electronic device that produces electromagnetic waves of certain wavelengths. Radio and television stations, for example, send an alternating current at a certain frequency to an antenna, producing a wave. These waves naturally spread out in the space around them, leading to the term "broadcasting." The waves are received by radio and television antennas in people's homes allowing them to enjoy broadcasts of music or television programs. Therefore, a radio is simply a radio wave detector that can select specific frequencies (which are marked as the radio station's position on the dial).

Radio waves have frequencies between 100 hertz and 1 billion hertz (or 1,000 megahertz). Most frequencies are measured in kilohertz (kHz) or megahertz (MHz) and are separated into bands (groups of frequencies) with different names—frequency modulated (FM), amplitude modulated (AM), very high frequency (VHF), and ultra high frequency (UHF), for example. In the United States, the Federal Communications Commission (FCC) decides which radio stations and which television stations are allowed to broadcast in certain frequencies.

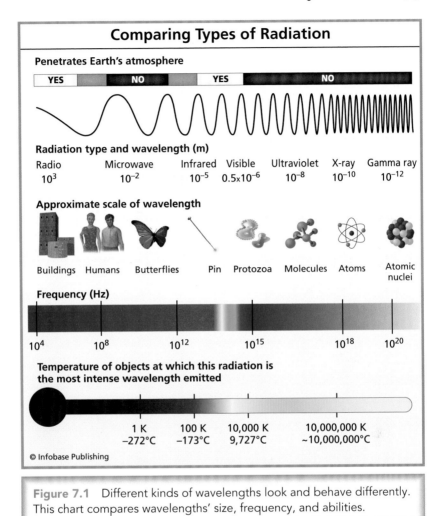

Comparing Types of Radiation

Penetrates Earth's atmosphere

| YES | NO | | YES | NO |

Radiation type and wavelength (m)

| Radio | Microwave | Infrared | Visible | Ultraviolet | X-ray | Gamma ray |
| 10^3 | 10^{-2} | 10^{-5} | 0.5×10^{-6} | 10^{-8} | 10^{-10} | 10^{-12} |

Approximate scale of wavelength

| Buildings | Humans | Butterflies | Pin | Protozoa | Molecules | Atoms | Atomic nuclei |

Frequency (Hz)

10^4 10^8 10^{12} 10^{15} 10^{18} 10^{20}

Temperature of objects at which this radiation is the most intense wavelength emitted

| 1 K | 100 K | 10,000 K | 10,000,000 K |
| −272°C | −173°C | 9,727°C | ~10,000,000°C |

© Infobase Publishing

Figure 7.1 Different kinds of wavelengths look and behave differently. This chart compares wavelengths' size, frequency, and abilities.

When a radio host announces that you are listening to 105.5 FM WDUV, for example, the announcer means that you are listening to a radio station broadcasting an FM radio signal at 105.5 megahertz with the call letters WDUV that was assigned to the station by the FCC. This means that the radio station's transmitter is producing electromagnetic waves with a frequency of 105,500,000 waves per second. All FM radio stations transmit signals between 88 and 108 megahertz. The FCC rules say that this range of frequencies may not be used for any other purpose other than FM radio broadcasts. Similarly, AM radio stations broadcast electromagnetic waves within a band of frequencies, as well. AM stations are limited to using frequencies between 535 kilohertz and 1.7 megahertz.

The UHF and VHF bands are mainly used for television broadcasting. Television channels 2 through 6, for example, use the frequencies 54 to 88 megahertz. Higher channels use 174 to 220 megahertz. Cell phones have their own frequencies, too (between 824 and 849 megahertz). In fact, every wireless device—garage door openers, cordless telephones, baby monitors, radio-controlled airplanes, and global positioning system (GPS) receivers, to name just a few examples—has its own little band of radio frequencies to work with.

Our wireless devices are not the only things that emit radio waves, however. Stars, sparks, and lightning do, too. This is why you may

Pump Up the Volume

Speakers in car and home stereo systems rely on electromagnets to work, too. To produce music, electronic sound recording machines must transform sound into an alternating current. Microphones perform this function. In some types of microphones, this is accomplished by having a flexible diaphragm attached to a coil of wire that surrounds a stationary magnet. As sound waves hit the diaphragm, the diaphragm and the attached coil of wire oscillate at frequencies that correspond to the sound being produced. This fluctuating movement induces an alternating current in the wire.

To play back the music, the alternating current must be transformed back into sound. When current moves though wires in a speaker, it moves magnets that are attached to fabric cones. When the current in the wire changes, the magnets move back and forth at different rates (or frequencies). This back-and-forth movement compresses air in front of the speaker cone, producing sound waves. The faster the cone moves back and forth, the higher the sound wave frequency and the higher pitched the sound. The speaker cone oscillates at the same frequency as the AC input, reproducing the music exactly.

hear static on your radio station during a thunderstorm. Static is also called interference because it interferes with radio wave reception.

MICROWAVES

Microwaves have shorter wavelengths and higher frequencies than radio waves. In fact, microwave wavelengths are usually only a few centimeters long. Like radio waves, microwaves are made by a transmitter. In a cellular telephone, the transmitter and antenna are on a computer chip. Inside a microwave oven, a device called a magnetron produces the electromagnetic waves.

Microwaves have a frequency of about 2.5 gigahertz (2.5 billion hertz). This electromagnetic frequency penetrates food very easily and heats it up, cooking it quickly. However, electromagnetic waves at this frequency are not absorbed by plastic, glass, or ceramics. Microwaves heat food up by causing atoms in the water and fats contained in the food to vibrate rapidly. When atoms move faster, their kinetic energy (the energy of motion) increases. The measurement of the average kinetic energy of an object is that object's **temperature**. Therefore, if the average kinetic energy increases, an object's temperature also increases.

Microwave ovens not only cause water and fat molecules to vibrate, they can also move free electrons back and forth fast enough to cause sparks. This is why it is not a good idea to put metals, which contain many free electrons, into a microwave oven. The sparks could start a fire.

INFRARED

Electromagnetic waves are a form of energy. They are sometimes called electromagnetic **radiation**. Radiation is defined as a form of energy that is given off in rays, waves, or particles. Infrared radiation (IR) was discovered by William Herschel (1738–1822) in 1800. The prefix *infra-* means below or beneath. On the electromagnetic spectrum, infrared waves are just below red visible light. Infrared waves have longer wavelengths and lower frequencies than visible light.

Scientists put infrared waves into two categories—near infrared and far infrared. Near IR waves have wavelengths closest to visible light. Far IR waves have wavelengths closer to microwaves. Our bodies perceive far IR waves as heat. These waves are given off by stars (including our Sun), lamps, and flames. In fact, anything that is warm—including your body—is giving off far infrared radiation. Some cameras, security sensors, and night-vision goggles can detect these IR waves. Far IR waves may also be used in medicine. Heat lamps may be used to help soothe a sports injury, for example.

Shorter near IR waves are popular for use in wireless remote control devices, which use IR signals to communicate with the appliances they control. Near IR waves are not hot. In medicine, doctors use near IR waves to measure how much oxygen is being carried by the blood and to diagnose certain diseases.

VISIBLE LIGHT

Our eyes can detect a part of the electromagnetic spectrum, too. However, visible light is just a small part of this spectrum. Specialized

Radar

One special use of radio waves is radar. Radar is a shorthand version of the phrase "radio detection and ranging." A radar transmitter sends out pulses of very high frequency radio waves or microwaves. These waves bounce off of objects, such as airplanes, ships, and cars. When the radar waves bounce off of an object, an echo is created—just as you hear the echo of your voice when you shout into a canyon. The radar echo returns to the radar dish and is displayed on a monitor. This is how a radar operator can tell where an object is. A computer measures the amount of time it takes for a radio wave to bounce back. This length of time shows how far away the object is. Radar can also be used to measure how fast a vehicle, such as a car, is going.

cells in our eyes, called rods and cones, are sensitive to electromagnetic waves with wavelengths between 400 and 700 nanometers (one billionth of a meter). When electromagnetic waves within the visible light range hit these specialized cells, they transmit an electrical signal to our brains. Our brains "decode" this information, which allows us to see. Within the narrow band of frequencies that comprise the visible light spectrum, our eyes perceive different frequencies as different colors. The lowest frequencies (closest to the frequencies of infrared) in the visible light spectrum are perceived as the color red, and the highest frequencies are seen as violet.

ULTRAVIOLET RADIATION

The shorter a wave's wavelength, the higher its frequency, and the greater the energy contained in the electromagnetic wave. This is the reason why ultraviolet (UV) rays, X-rays, and gamma rays can damage the human body—there is a lot of energy contained in these waves.

Like infrared radiation, scientists have divided ultraviolet radiation into different categories—near UV, far UV, and extreme UV. Near UV waves have wavelengths closest to visible light. Extreme UV waves are closer in wavelength to X-rays and gamma rays. Extreme UV waves have the most energy of all UV waves. The wavelengths of far UV waves are between these two.

The Sun gives off electromagnetic waves of all different wavelengths, including the visible range, infrared, and ultraviolet. About 7% of the radiation given off by the Sun is in the UV range. This is the part of sunlight that is responsible for sunburns and suntans. Suntans are the result of a chemical process in the skin triggered by UV radiation. Tanning beds and lights also emit UV radiation to trigger the same chemical reaction. Over a lifetime, overexposure to UV radiation can cause damage to the DNA inside skin cells and result in skin cancer.

Luckily, Earth's atmosphere shields us from much of the Sun's UV radiation. About 12 to 24 miles (20 to 40 km) above the surface of Earth, there is a relatively high concentration of oxygen molecules that have three oxygen atoms that are chemically bonded together (O_3). O_3 is called ozone. This region of the atmosphere is appropriately called the ozone layer. The ozone layer protects the living organisms on Earth by absorbing most of the UV radiation that comes from the Sun. That is why, in 1974, scientists were alarmed when they found that certain chemicals called chlorofluorocarbons (CFCs) could chemically break apart ozone molecules. At the time, CFCs were used as refrigerants in refrigerators and air conditioning units and as propellants in spray cans. Concern over how depletion of the ozone layer could affect humans and other life on Earth led policy makers around the world to sign the 1987 Montreal Protocol. The leaders that signed this international agreement pledged to decrease their country's use and production of substances that could destroy the ozone layer and seriously endanger human health through increased exposure to the Sun's UV rays.

Still, UV radiation is not all bad. Hospitals often use UV lamps to kill bacteria and viruses on surgical equipment and in operating rooms. Food and drug companies also use these lamps to eliminate these microbes from their products.

X-RAYS AND GAMMA RAYS

The X-ray was discovered by accident by Wilhelm Röntgen (1845–1923) in 1895. He called them X-rays because he did not know exactly how these rays were made and how they worked. (The letter "X" is often used in mathematics to represent an unknown.) X-rays have shorter wavelengths than UV waves have. Therefore, X-rays also have more energy. Along with blocking some of the UV waves emitted by the Sun, Earth's atmosphere also deflects almost all X-rays coming in from space and prevents them from reaching the surface.

One of the most common uses of X-rays is taking pictures of the inside of the body in order to diagnose certain medical problems. For example, bombarding different areas of the body with X-ray radiation can reveal the existence of broken bones or cavities in teeth. Tissues inside the human body that contain elements with relatively large atomic numbers, such as calcium, tend to absorb more electromagnetic waves in the frequencies of X-rays than tissues that contain lighter elements such as carbon, hydrogen, and oxygen. When a doctor orders an X-ray, a beam of X-rays is sent

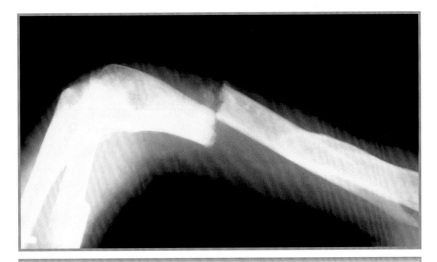

Figure 7.2 X-rays are typically negative film images, wherein areas that are exposed to more light appear darker. Hard material, such as bone, appears white, and soft material will look black or gray. Technicians can bring different materials into focus by varying the intensity of the X-ray beam.

through a patient's body and onto a piece of X-ray film. The X-rays pass easily through soft tissue and hit the film, turning it black. X-rays do not pass through bones and teeth as well, however, and so the film stays white or light gray in those areas. X-rays will not pass through a lead apron either. Lead aprons are used by X-ray technicians and dentists to protect parts of the body that do not need to be exposed to the X-rays.

Gamma rays are the electromagnetic waves with the highest frequency and the highest energy. Gamma rays are emitted naturally by radioactive elements such as radium and uranium. These rays can also be produced artificially in nuclear power plants and particle accelerators. Exposure to gamma rays can kill living cells. They can also pass through most materials and can be difficult to block.

X-rays and gamma rays can be harmful to humans because they are forms of ionizing radiation. Ionizing radiation produces ions that can pass through matter—including the human body. When these charged ions hit atoms inside the body, they can rip electrons away from atoms and leave behind charged particles. This process can break chemical bonds inside the body, thereby breaking down molecules that are necessary for proper functioning. Ionizing radiation can kill or mutate (damage) cells. Mutated cells can turn into cancer cells.

Because X-rays and gamma rays can kill living cells, however, they can also be used to treat cancer when used in a controlled manner. This type of treatment is called radiation therapy or radiotherapy. Radiotherapy works because ionizing radiation is especially harmful to cells that divide quickly. Because cancer cells divide much faster than normal, healthy cells, radiotherapy kills more cancer cells than it does healthy cells. However, radiotherapy does kill some healthy cells (especially those that naturally divide faster than other normal cells), and so it results in some of the side effects of cancer treatment. For example, the cells of the stomach lining are constantly dying off and being replaced. When radiotherapy damages the rapidly dividing cells of the stomach lining, the patient often feels nauseous (meaning sick to their stomach). Radiotherapy can also damage hair follicles, causing the patient's hair to fall out. Once radiotherapy is complete, however, most of these symptoms go away. The patient's hair even grows back.

Harnessing Electromagnetism

As we've discussed, people use electricity, electromagnets, and electromagnetic waves in many areas of our everyday lives. So, how does the energy that we use get from the electric power plants that produce it into our homes, schools, and businesses?

ELECTRICITY AT HOME

Power is transferred from an electrical power plant to our homes using a huge network of wires and other equipment that is collectively called the power grid. This distribution grid starts at the power plant where giant spinning electrical generators are housed. Many different power sources can be used to make these electrical generators spin. For example, in a hydroelectric dam like the Hoover Dam, which is located on the border of Nevada and Arizona, water turns a large wheel called a turbine. A turbine is a device that converts the flow of a fluid (air, water, steam, or other gas) into mechanical energy that can be used to generate electricity. Windmills, also called wind turbines, use the power of the wind to spin the generator. Still, most electrical power plants use steam to turn the turbines. The steam can be produced by burning coal, oil, or natural gas. It can

Figure 8.1 Built by thousands of people during the Great Depression, the Hoover Dam holds back the Colorado River.

also be produced by the heat generated by nuclear reactions that occur in a nuclear reactor.

The turning turbines are attached by a metal shaft to the electric generators. Remember that electric generators contain the same components an electric motor does—including magnets and coils of wire—and can convert the mechanical energy created by the spinning generator into electrical energy. The electricity generated at the power plant leaves the plant through large power lines and winds up at a transmission substation.

Transformers

The transmission substation contains devices called transformers. Transformers can convert electricity from one voltage to another voltage. The voltage of the electricity coming from the power plant is at about 25,000 volts. In order for the current to travel over long distances, the voltage needs to be boosted to about 400,000 volts. The electricity must be transmitted at such high voltages in order

Photovoltaic Effect

You may have noticed some calculators have solar cells. These calculators need no batteries. Many of them do not even have an off switch. As long as there is enough light, the calculator works. You may have also heard about the need to find sources of renewable energy to make electricity. Wind power and water power are types of renewable energy that can be used to turn large turbines in power plants. Sunlight is another source of renewable energy, but solar panels produce electricity differently. The small, dark cells in a solar-powered calculator and the larger cells that make up solar panels can also be called photovoltaic cells. Photovoltaic cells convert sunlight directly into electricity.

Photovoltaic cells are made of a semiconductor (usually silicon). When sunlight hits the silicon, some of the electromagnetic wave's energy is absorbed by the semiconductor. This energy knocks electrons in the silicon loose and allows them to move freely. Electric fields in the photovoltaic cell force the electrons to flow in a particular direction, creating an electric current, which can be collected and used to do work—like powering a calculator or heating a home.

to minimize heat loss. Remember that the higher the current, the greater the heat loss. Because the relationship between current and voltage is inversely proportional, if the current is low, then the voltage must be high. This high-voltage electricity is carried over our towns and cities in large wires supported by metal columns called pylons.

Homes and businesses cannot use electricity at 400,000 volts. The voltage must first be "stepped down." This procedure is also performed by a transformer. Transformers are made by placing two electromagnets side by side, but not touching. When an alternating current moves through one of the coils (called the primary coil) a magnetic field that changes with the changing voltage is produced. The changing magnetic field in the primary coil moves across the second coil (called the secondary coil), inducing an alternating current.

The voltages produced in the two coils are proportional to the number of turns in each coil. If the secondary coil has more turns than the primary coil, the voltage will be higher in the secondary coil. This type of transformer is called a step-up transformer because it converts low voltages to higher voltages. On the other hand, if there are more turns in the primary coil, the primary coil will have a higher voltage than the secondary coil. When the voltage is reduced at the transformer, the transformer is called a step-down transformer. Depending on where you live, there may be step-down transformers near the edge of your city that drop the voltage carried through the high-voltage power lines to a lower 2,300 volts. In the event of a downed power line, this stepped-down voltage is relatively safer than 400,000 volts. Other step-down transformers throughout the city drop the voltage to 120 volts so it can be safely used in people's homes. If the power lines in your neighborhood run above the ground, you may have noticed a step-down transformer attached to one of the utility poles (it looks like a bucket attached to the side of the pole). In many neighborhoods, however, power lines are buried underground. In these neighborhoods, the step-down transformers are often housed in a green transformer box between every house or two.

Because DC power supplies produce a steady magnetic field, not an alternating (or changing) one, a direct current would not

Figure 8.2 Workers clean a large transformer in the powerhouse at the Grand Coulee Dam in Washington State.

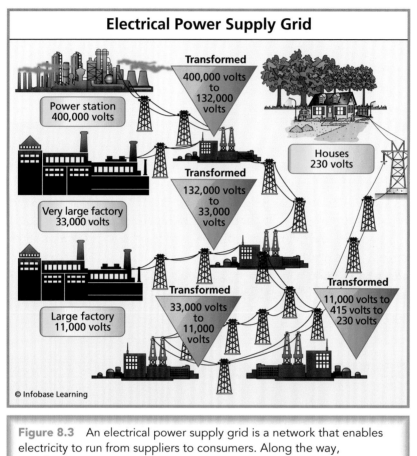

Electrical Power Supply Grid

Power station
400,000 volts

Transformed
400,000 volts
to
132,000
volts

Houses
230 volts

Very large factory
33,000 volts

Transformed
132,000 volts
to
33,000
volts

Large factory
11,000 volts

Transformed
33,000 volts
to
11,000
volts

Transformed
11,000 volts to
415 volts to
230 volts

© Infobase Learning

Figure 8.3 An electrical power supply grid is a network that enables electricity to run from suppliers to consumers. Along the way, transformers increase or decrease the supply of electrical current.

induce a current in the secondary coil. Therefore, transformers will not work with DC.

Fuses and Circuit Breakers

When you plug in a new appliance, lamp, or computer, you are adding a new device to a parallel circuit. Every time a new electronic device is plugged in, more current is needed to run it. Therefore, a higher current is drawn through the wires of the house. Too much current going through wires that are not designed to carry that much current can start an electrical fire. To prevent this from happening, all homes should have a fuse or circuit breaker box.

Fuses contain thin metal strips inside them, similar to the filament in a light bulb. The metal in the fuse has a particular melting point, and if the current coming though the fuse exceeds the amount of current that the wire can handle, the metal heats up to its melting point and breaks. When this happens, the fuse is "blown." A blown fuse breaks the circuit. To get current flowing again, the fuse must be replaced.

A circuit breaker is a switch that automatically switches to the off position if the current coming though the breaker is higher than a preset level. To get the current flowing again, the switch needs to be reset to the on position. If blown fuses and tripped circuit breakers are a common problem, the home's wiring should be checked.

Because every device that is plugged in increases the amount of current that must flow through the circuit, using a plug extender to allow you to plug more things into one outlet is not the best idea. If the fuses or circuit breakers malfunction, you could easily overload the circuit and cause a fire.

SUPERCONDUCTORS

Scientists are always looking for better, cleaner, and less expensive ways to produce electricity. In 1911, a Dutch physicist named Heike Kamerlingh Onnes (1853–1926) discovered that if he made mercury cold enough, an electric current would flow though the metal with no resistance at all. Onnes named this phenomenon superconductivity. The mercury had to be cooled to a chilly -452°F (-269°C) to make it work, however. No resistance means that no energy is lost to heating. With no resistance and no energy loss, once a current starts flowing though a superconductor, the current could, theoretically, flow for years without the help of an outside power source.

When a strong magnet is placed near a superconductor, the magnet becomes suspended in mid-air over the superconductor. This phenomenon is known as the Meissner-Ochsenfeld effect. Using this effect, engineers have successfully made passenger trains that are called magnetic levitation monorails, or "maglev" trains. Because these trains do not contact the ground, they are fast, quiet, smooth, and easier to maintain than conventional trains. Scientists also use the Meissner-Ochsenfeld effect to determine whether or not a substance is in a superconducting state because it is easier to test for levitating magnets than it is to test for zero resistance.

During Onnes's time, mercury was considered to be a perfect conductor of electricity. Since then, however, hundreds of superconducting elements, compounds, and metal alloys have been found. However, like mercury, they only become superconductors at very low temperatures. While it would be a great idea to use superconductors wherever we need electricity because of the large amount of energy they save, they are not about to take the place of standard conducting materials (such as metals) in household wires because of the low temperatures required for using them. In the 1960s, however, some superconductors were made, mostly using an alloy of the elements niobium and tin, which are practical enough to be used widely in science and medicine because they do not need to reach such low temperatures to exhibit zero resistance.

If the wire used to make an electromagnet is made out of a superconducting material, the result is a superconducting electromagnet. Superconducting electromagnets are the strongest magnets yet made. Doctors make use of superconducting electromagnets in a

Buried Treasure

Whether they are used to find valuables dropped in the sand by careless tourists, or used by airport security to find hidden weapons, metal detectors create electromagnetic fields. In the most common type of metal detector, called a very low frequency (VLF) metal detector, electricity is sent through a transmitter coil, first in one direction and then in the opposite direction. The current switches direction thousands of times a second. This current produces a magnetic field. This magnetic field induces a current within any conductive material, such as the metal of a watch or a gun, for example. The induced current causes the conductive material to give off its own magnetic field, which, in turn, induces a current in the receiver coil of the metal detector. This current passes through a control box that produces an audible signal that indicates the detector has found something conductive.

magnetic resonance imaging (MRI) machine. A MRI machine can take highly detailed pictures of the inside of the human body, similar to an X-ray machine. MRIs, however, can sometimes show tumors that will not show up on an X-ray. Because MRIs rely on extremely strong magnets, however, people with pacemakers, steel pins or rods, or other metal parts inside their bodies cannot get MRIs because the magnets could cause the metal to shift inside the body, causing internal injuries.

Because the first superconductors required the use of liquefied helium, their use was severely limited. Liquid helium requires specialized equipment to keep it cold and liquefied, and it is expensive. In 1987, however, scientists found a new type of superconducting material that only needed to be cooled to -297.7°F (-183.1°C). Fairly quickly afterwards they found a material that would work at -207.7°F (-133.2°C). These new materials could be cooled using liquid nitrogen, a much more inexpensive and common source than liquid helium. There is a downside to these new materials, however. They are brittle and, therefore, hard to shape into wires without breaking them. They also cannot carry very high electric currents, and strong magnetic fields disturb the way they work. These problems would have to be overcome before they could be widely used.

PARTICLE ACCELERATORS

Scientists use superconducting electromagnets to study the effects of magnetic fields on objects. These electromagnets are also used in particle accelerators to direct the movements of high-speed charged particles. Scientists use experimental particle accelerators to study atomic, nuclear, and elementary particle physics. In accelerators such as the Tevatron at the Fermi National Accelerator Laboratory near Chicago, Illinois, and the Large Hadron Collider (LHC) near Geneva, Switzerland, scientists keep positively-charged particles moving rapidly in one direction and negatively-charged particles circulating in the opposite direction.

When allowed to meet, the violent collisions between these particles, moving at almost the speed of light, can give scientists new insights into the elementary particles and the fundamental forces at work in nature. The LHC, at 16.8 miles (27 km) in circumference, is

Figure 8.4   CERN's Large Hadron Collider near Geneva, Switzerland, is the world's largest particle accelerator.

the largest particle accelerator built to date. In addition to research, particle accelerators also have a practical purpose. Some large hospitals have their own particle accelerators that they use to produce radioactive isotopes for cancer treatment.

MAGNETIC BOTTLES

Scientists are researching other ways to use magnetic fields, too. One avenue of research they are pursuing is using a magnetic field to contain high-temperature plasmas. If scientists are able to figure out how to harness these high-temperature plasmas, they could be used in nuclear fusion reactors. At present, most nuclear power plants use nuclear fission instead of nuclear fusion to generate the energy to heat water to make steam and turn turbines to produce electricity. However, fusion reactions would be better because they produce less radioactive waste and the fuel lasts longer.

The problem with fusion is that getting atomic nuclei to fuse and generate energy requires very high temperatures. For example, in order to get hydrogen particles to fuse together, hydrogen plasma needs to be heated to 180,000,032°F (100 million°C). Material this hot cannot be stored in any type of metal or glass container because the containers would melt. However, because plasmas are made up of charged particles, scientists can use magnetic fields to hold the plasmas in what they call a "magnetic bottle." Research is ongoing.

THE IMPACT

People do not usually dwell on how much their everyday lives rely on the flow of electricity. Just for a moment, imagine what might happen in the event of a complete and total blackout. Televisions, radios, cordless telephones, and computers would not work. Cell phones might work, but you would not be able to recharge their batteries,

Conducting Plastic

Scientists have long understood that plastics do not conduct electricity. In fact, plastics are used to coat the electrical wires on most of the appliances in our homes for that very reason. However, scientists Alan J. Heeger, Alan G. Mac-Diarmid, and Hideri Shirakawa found that certain plastics, modified in specific ways, could be turned from excellent insulators into conductors. These scientists were awarded the 2000 Nobel Prize in chemistry for their discovery.

Called electroactive polymers (EAPs), these plastics change shape when an electric current is applied to them. More importantly, they can also produce an electrical current when their shape is changed. One way scientists hope to use this new material is to make the soles of hiking boots. The idea is that as a hiker walks and the sole of the boot flexes, the electric current produced by the EAP could be used, for example, to recharge batteries or to power a flashlight. Other scientists are hoping to use EAPs as replacement muscles for people who have been paralyzed or for the moving parts of robots.

so they would not work for long. Air conditioners, heating systems, refrigerators, and most stoves and ovens would not work either.

Because there would be no traffic lights, driving would become extremely hazardous. Driving would be short-lived, as well, because most gas stations rely on electric pumps to bring the fuel up from underground tanks to supply the gas pumps. Even if you were able to get to where you were going, you probably could not buy anything anyway. Credit card machines and automatic teller machines (ATMs) do not work without electricity. Without computers, bank tellers would not be able to supply you with cash either.

Electricity and electromagnetism (especially in the form of the electric motor) literally changed the face of the world. When the electric motor was invented, people could all of a sudden ride upward in elevator cars instead having to hike up an unmanageable number of steps, and the skylines of Manhattan and Chicago would never be the same again. People no longer had to live and work in the same place, either. They could travel to work by car. Houses were built farther and farther from the center of downtown areas, leading to the birth of suburban sprawl. People became mobile, and therefore, could meet more and different people. This change was reflected in the composition of the American family. Before the invention of electric streetcars and the automobile, most people met the person that they would marry in their own neighborhood. However, in a mobile society, people can meet and marry anyone of any background. Communication in the form of the telegraph, the telephone, and, finally, the computer has allowed companies to sell their products and to buy their supplies from halfway around the world. Electric lights made it possible to work, read, and do things after dark. Without a doubt, the scientists who discovered how electric and magnetic fields worked and the men and women who invented ways to harness these fields have changed our world forever.

Glossary

atom   The basic building block of all matter

circuit   A circular path in which current can flow

conductor   A substance that charged particles flow through easily

current   The movement of electric charges from one place to another

diode   A device that will only allow current to flow in one direction

electrode   The point where electrons enter or leave a battery

electrolyte   A substance capable of conducting electricity when dissolved or melted

electromagnet   A temporary magnet in which the magnetic field is produced by a flow of electric current.

electromagnetic induction   Producing an electric current by changing a magnetic field

electron   A negatively charged subatomic particle that travels around an atom's nucleus on energy levels

ferromagnetic   Materials that can become magnetic when exposed to a magnetic field

insulator   A substance that charged particles cannot flow through easily

ion   A charged particle created when an atom loses or gains electrons

kinetic energy   The energy of motion

matter   Anything that has mass and takes up space

neutron   Electrically neutral subatomic particle found in an atom's nucleus

nucleus   The dense, central core of an atom

ohms   The measure of the amount of resistance a current encounters as it moves through a circuit.

potential energy   An object's capacity for doing work due to its position

power   The rate at which work is done

proton   Positively charged subatomic particle found in an atom's nucleus

radiation   Energy that is given off in rays, waves, or particles

resistance   The degree to which a material slows down the flow of electrons

semiconductor   A substance that can act as either a conductor or an insulator

solenoid   A coil of insulated current-carrying wire that produces a magnetic field

superconductor   A material that has almost no resistance to electrical current at very low temperatures

temperature   The measurement of the average kinetic energy of the atoms in an object

valence electron   An electron on the highest, or outermost, energy level of an atom

watt   A unit of electrical power

Bibliography

Bodanis, David. *Electric Universe: The Shocking True Story of Electricity.* New York, NY: Crown Publishers, 2005.

Bord, Donald and Vern Ostdiek. *Inquiry Into Physics.* 4th edition. Pacific Grove, Calif: Brooks/Cole, 2000.

Brain, Marshall. "How Semiconductors Work." How Stuff Works. Available online. http://electronics.howstuffworks.com/diode.htm. Accessed Aug. 27, 2008.

California Energy Commission. "Electricity Transmission System." Available online. http://www.energyquest.ca.gov/story/chapter07.html. Accessed Aug. 27, 2008.

California Energy Commission. "Nuclear Energy: Fission and Fusion." Available online. http://www.energyquest.ca.gov/story/chapter13.html. Accessed Aug. 28, 2008.

De Pree, Christopher. *Physics Made Simple.* New York, NY: Broadway Books, 2004.

Freudenrich, Craig. "How Nerves Work." How Stuff Works. Available online. http://health.howstuffworks.com/nerve.htm. Accessed Aug. 25, 2008.

Georgia State University. "Ferromagnetism." Available online. http://hyperphysics.phy-astr.gsu.edu/hbase/solids/ferro.html. Accessed Aug. 26, 2008.

Hebrew University of Jerusalem. "Charles-François de Cisternay Du Fay." Apr. 12, 2003. Available online. http://chem.ch.huji.ac.il/history/du_fay.html. Accessed Aug. 25, 2008.

Hipschman, Ron. "Lightning." San Francisco Exploratorium. Available online. http://www.exploratorium.edu/ronh/weather/weather.html. Accessed Aug. 25, 2008.

Hsu, Jeremy. "Sloshing Inside Earth Changes Protective Magnetic Field." Aug. 18, 2008. Available online. http://www.space.com/scienceastronomy/080818-mm-earth-core.html. Accessed Aug. 26, 2008.

Kleiner, Kurt. "Nuclear Fusion Plasma Problem Tackled." New Scientist Technology. May 22, 2006. Available online. http://technology. newscientist.com/article/dn9202-nuclear-fusion-plasma-problem-tackled.html. Accessed Aug. 29, 2008.

Lewin, Walter. "8.02 Electricity and Magnetism." MIT OpenCourseWare. Available online. http://ocw.mit.edu/ocwweb/physics/8-02electricity-and-magnetismspring2002/coursehome/. Accessed Aug. 25, 2008.

Moring, Gary. *The Complete Idiot's Guide to Understanding Einstein.* Indianapolis, Ind.: Macmillan USA, Inc., 2000.

National Aeronautics and Space Administration. "NASA Satellites Discover What Powers Northern Lights." July 24, 2008. Available online. http://www.nasa.gov/home/hqnews/2008/jul/hq_08185_themis.html. Accessed Aug. 26, 2008.

National Geographic Society. "Electric Eel." Available online. http://animals. nationalgeographic.com/animals/fish/electric-eel.html. Accessed Aug. 25, 2008.

National High Magnetic Field Laboratory. "Mag Lab U: Learn about Electricity and Magnetism." Available online. http://www.magnet.fsu.edu/ education/. Accessed Aug. 25, 2008.

Parker, Barry. *Science 101: Physics.* New York, NY: HarperCollins, 2007.

Tyson, Jeff. "How Metal Detectors Work." How Stuff Works. Available online. http://electronics.howstuffworks.com/metal-detector.htm. Accessed Aug. 29, 2008.

University of Tennessee. "The Earth's Magnetic Field." Available online. http://csep10.phys.utk.edu/astr161/lect/earth/magnetic.html. Accessed Aug. 26, 2008.

Wilber, Scott. "What is a Short Circuit?" Available online. http://www. physlink.com/education/askexperts/ae470.cfm. Accessed Aug. 26, 2008.

Zavisa, John. "How Lightning Works." How Stuff Works. Available online. http://science.howstuffworks.com/lightning.htm. Accessed Aug. 25, 2008.

Zavisa, John. "How Van de Graaff Generators Work." How Stuff Works. Available online. http://science.howstuffworks.com/vdg.htm. Accessed Aug. 25, 2008.

Further Resources

Cobb, Vicki. *Sources of Forces: Science Fun with Force Fields*. Minneapolis, Minn.: Lerner Publishing Group, 2007.

Colbert, David. *Thomas Edison*. New York, NY: Simon & Schuster Children's Publishing, 2008.

Fairley, Peter. *Electricity and Magnetism*. Minneapolis, Minn.: Twenty-First Century Books, 2007.

Gardner, Robert. *Energizing Science Projects with Electricity and Magnetism*. Berkeley Heights, NJ: Enslow Publishers, 2006.

Lynette, Rachel. *Electrical Experiments: Electricity and Circuits*. Chicago, Ill.: Heinemann, 2008.

Parker, Steve. *Electricity and Magnetism*. Milwaukee, Wisc.: Gareth Stevens Publishing, 2007.

Smuskiewicz, Alfred. *Magnets and Electromagnetism*. Chicago, Ill.: Heinemann, 2007.

Solway, Andrew. *Exploring Electricity and Magnetism*. New York, NY: Rosen Publishing Group, 2007.

Spangler, Steve. *Secret Science: 25 Science Experiments Your Teacher Doesn't Know About*. Sandy, UT: Silverleaf Press, 2007.

Spilsbury, Richard and Louise Spilsbury. *What Is Electricity and Magnetism?: Exploring Science with Hands-on Activities*. Berkeley Heights, NJ: Enslow Publishers, 2008.

Tomecek, Stephen. *Scientific American: Electromagnetism, and How It Works*. New York, NY: Chelsea House Publishers, 2007.

Web Sites

Energy Story

http://www.energyquest.ca.gov/story/index.html

The California Energy Commission Web site provides information on many different types of energy, including static electricity, electric circuits, and electric power plants.

Energy Information Administration Kid's Page

http://www.eia.doe.gov/kids/energyfacts/sources/electricity.html

The U.S. Energy Information Administration has put together a Web page that includes information on the basics of electricity, renewable and nonrenewable resources, and using and saving energy.

Exploratorium: Magnetism & Energy

http://www.exploratorium.edu/snacks/iconmagnetism.html
http://www.exploratorium.edu/snacks/iconelectricity.html

The California Exploratorium site has several magnetism and electricity experiments you can try at home. Each experiment comes with explanations of how and why the experiment works.

Jefferson Lab: How to Make an Electromagnet

http://education.jlab.org/qa/electromagnet.html

The Jefferson Lab explains how to make an electromagnet out of common hardware store materials.

Magnet Man

http://www.coolmagnetman.com/magindex.htm

The Magnet Man explains the basics of magnetism and provides many experiments that can be done with magnets.

PBS: Edison's Miracle of Light

http://www.pbs.org/wgbh/amex/edison/

This companion Web site to the PBS film of the same name provides a transcript of the program as well as special features such as a time line of Thomas Edison's life and downloadable recordings produced by the Edison Company between 1888 and 1929.

PBS: Transistorized!

http://www.pbs.org/transistor/

This site provides the complete story of the development of the transistor.

Physics4Kids

http://www.physics4kids.com/files/elec_intro.html

Physics4Kids explains electric and magnetic fields, current, resistance, and DC and AC power in easy-to-understand language.

Picture Credits

Index

About the Author

Kristi Lew is the author of more than 30 science books for teachers and young people. Fascinated with science from a young age, she studied biochemistry and genetics at North Carolina State University. Before she started writing full time, she worked in genetic laboratories and taught high-school science. When she's not writing, she enjoys sailing with her husband aboard their small sailboat, *Proton*. She lives, writes, and sails in Florida, the lightning capital of the United States.